grapher
2010
from Dave and June

GHOST ISLAND

ISLE OF WIGHT GHOSTS
BOOK FIVE

GAY BALDWIN

Copyright © Gay Baldwin 2000

First published November 2000

Reprinted 2004

Published by Gay Baldwin,
9 Pine Tree Close,
Cowes,
Isle of Wight
PO31 8DX

Distributed by Gay Baldwin
Telephone (01983) 294651
e-mail: gb@hauntediw.demon.co.uk
website: www.ghost-island.com

Cover photograph and design by Patrick Eden.
Text set by IW Council Printing Services.
Printed by Short Run Press, Exeter.

ISBN 0-9520062-8-6

CONTENTS

INTRODUCTION

Almost everybody knows at least one ghost story - or knows a friend or relative who does. Sightings of ghosts, spirits, phantoms, poltergeists, call them what you will, have been reported from all over the world as long as people have been around.

I have been collecting and researching stories of ghosts and hauntings here on the Isle of Wight for almost 25 years, and during that time I have moved from sceptic to believer. The weight of evidence is too overwhelming to be dismissed.

Although every haunting is different, there are certain marked similarities running through the various accounts. For example, many ghosts seem fascinated by small trinkets, keys, coins and jewellery, which then disappear for days or sometimes months on end. Others are attracted to electrical equipment, occasionally making use of the power in some unknown way, and running up huge electricity bills in the process!

So how do we perceive or experience ghosts? Our main senses of sight, hearing, smell, taste and touch are actually very limited. Ghostly phenomena are generally seen, heard or smelled. So where does this information come from?

From the imagination, some would say, thus dismissing all reports of hauntings and supernatural activity out of hand. "There's no such thing as ghosts," they insist. "It's all in the mind," they cry. But these days such folk are increasingly in the minority. Belief in the supernatural, a willingness to keep an open mind and explore the possibility that maybe there is something else 'out there' is refreshingly apparent.

Today there is a considerable and growing interest in ghosts and hauntings. More and more people are willing to talk about 'their' ghosts and to admit to having had a supernatural experience. In fact the overwhelming majority of ghosts and hauntings are benign, if not downright friendly. But if an apparition or troublesome spirit troubles you, there are a number of psychics and people who can help to 'move it on'. Contact me for further details.

In broad terms, a ghost or spirit can be described as the life force of someone who has died, or passed on, but for any number of reasons, has not ceased to exist in this realm. Often ghosts are the spirits or souls of those who have died violently or suddenly, well before their time. Others become ghosts because they are somehow trapped on the earth plane, unable to accept that they have died; or have become lost on their way to the afterlife. A few retain such strong ties to the living, or to some aspect of their former life that they cannot bear to move on. However the dimension in which they exist is timeless, and does not seem to be governed by our concept of time. When contacted through mediums and psychics, these spirits are often unaware - and surprised to discover how long they have been dead.

However, some hauntings are clearly little more than a kind of psychic video recording on the fabric or atmosphere of a building or place. This results in the mindless repetition of an event or a moment in time, which replays in an endless loop to anyone who is on the right wavelength or 'channel' to see or hear it.

Imagine this: in the space occupied by your body now are all the frequencies of the radio and television stations in the area. You can't see them. They can't see each other even though they share the same space, because they are on different wavelengths. Tune in to one of those stations and that's the one you will hear. The frequency becomes that station's reality. Move the dial to another station and the radio's reality alters. It is the same for people. At the moment we are tuned to this wavelength, but when we die our soul or spirit moves to a different wavelength. Perhaps what we call 'ghosts' are spirits on other wavelengths.

So do unseen dimensions of reality exist around us? Just because our very restricted senses cannot readily tune in to them does not mean that there's nothing out there. The eyes of humans are designed to pick up a very limited range of information signals and colours. Sounds are simply waves or vibrations which are detected by a mechanism in our ear, amplifying the vibrations which are interpreted by the brain. However, we know that many other creatures around us such as dogs, cats and bats have much more sensitive sight and hearing than we do, and can see and hear things we cannot. Scientific instruments confirm this.

When a ghostly figure is seen apparently walking through a 'solid' wall, can we believe our own eyes? Perhaps we can. For nothing in the universe is really solid. All matter is actually made up of countless tiny molecules vibrating at differing and incredible speeds. Objects we perceive as being solid, such as walls, furniture, even this book, are in reality, energy vibrating at different wavelengths which creates visible patterns. Quantum physics and mathematical theories have supported this idea for some time. When asked to define matter, the great Albert Einstein described it as "congealed light". Taken to their ultimate, matter and energy are one and the same.

So, do ghosts exist, albeit in a dimension or on a wavelength different to our own? I believe that they do. I have, over the years, interviewed many hundreds of people from all walks of life, who have seen, heard, felt, or even smelled ghosts. Some of the strange events and occurrences would have been all but impossible to make up. Now I challenge you to read these stories and make up your own mind.

As the noted author H.P.Lovecraft wrote:

"There is something marvellous beyond the horizon of death and the limit of our sight. It becomes personal knowledge when our minds are coaxed out of the shadows of the purely material world and into the brilliance and brightness of the world of spirit .... that lies just beyond the limit of our sight."

East and West Cowes in early Victorian times

Chapter One

ENTITIES AT EAST COWES

HORROR AT CLARENCE ROAD

A young mother and her baby daughter escaped from a terrifying presence at their East Cowes home in the middle of the night, in an incident reminiscent of the film 'The Amityville Horror'.

Despite the intervention of a local priest, who twice tried to rid the house in Clarence Road of the entity, Laura Lumley and 15-month-old Danielle could no longer stand the haunting; the ghostly footsteps; moving furniture and extreme temperature changes, which seemed to originate in the baby's room. Things became so bad one September night in 1993, that Laura grabbed the baby and ran from the house.

Laura's stepfather, Graham Cant, lives just round the corner from the detached two-storey house, built a few years after the end of the last war. He, too, experienced the weird and disturbing events there over a period of several weeks.

As a soldier in the Army, Laura's husband Paul (the couple are now divorced) was often away from home and it had been left to her to rent a house for them on the Island. But right from the start, Laura had her doubts about this one. "I did not feel comfortable but I put the unfriendly atmosphere down to the fact that it was empty and unfurnished. The first two days when I was there on my own it was fine; the trouble only started when Danielle arrived."

Although the baby's room was carpeted, Laura would hear footsteps running round the room overhead on bare floorboards. This usually started at 7.30pm and continued intermittently until 10pm. Although she went upstairs many times to investigate, Laura could never discover what was causing the noises, although she could see small footprints appearing in the pile of the carpet.

Baby Danielle meanwhile, would happily sit and play with the unseen presence, share her toys, chatter to it and play peek-a-boo. Occasionally the toddler would cry out, "Mine, mine, mine" when her ghostly playmate snatched a toy from her. Whatever the presence was, it was clearly quite obsessed with the baby and one morning even got her ready for her bath. Laura recalls, "I went into Danielle's room to find she was wearing just her nappy. Her pyjamas had been taken off and were lying on the end of the bed, buttoned and folded."

After this, Laura asked her local priest to bless the house, but his intervention only seemed to make matters worse. An alcove in Danielle's room always felt icy cold and at times this penetrating chill would permeate the whole room. Laura had almost persuaded herself that she was imagining things when those running footsteps started one night when Graham was in the house. He shot upstairs to see what was happening, in time to observe Danielle's baby-walker move across the room on its own. After this, everyday objects started to go missing. Scissors and belts would disappear, and one evening as Laura was using the computer, she glimpsed a tall shadowy figure with a large head move past the door.

"At first I just ignored it, but then I heard a soft scuffing noise. It was Danielle's Mr Blobby toy sliding across the floor towards me," said Laura. When Paul came home on leave, he too, noticed the strange happenings, and sometimes heard the sound of sobbing. This might have been put down to his imagination - except that Graham also heard the noise, and it was somehow recorded on Laura's telephone answering machine.

There was sometimes a very strong smell of toast in the house and at night, when the baby was in bed, the front room would grow unbearably hot, lights would flicker and banging noises would start. After one particularly disturbed night, Laura rang the priest in a panic at 3am, begging him to come round immediately.

"I could hear someone trying to open the bathroom door and footsteps walking up and down outside my bedroom door. That bathroom felt very cold and I always had the impression that I was being watched in there."

An Evil Presence

"The priest told me that there was an evil presence in the bedrooms and commanded whatever was in the house to leave immediately. But two days later, it was back again."

One Sunday night when Graham and his teenage son Gavin were in the house with Laura, they all heard a tremendous bang. "It sounded like an explosion upstairs. The whole house seemed to shake and I really thought the roof had fallen in," Graham said. However, a quick check showed nothing was out of place and neighbours had heard nothing at all. By this time Laura, who was at the end of her tether, decided to move out. She told the letting agents that the house was haunted and they quickly found her another house. She was packed and ready to go in record time.

However, that East Cowes house was not ready to let her or Danielle go without a fight.

"I really thought things would be alright at first," said Graham, who stayed in the house for that last night with a sleeping bag on the floor. "But just before midnight the footsteps started in the baby's room. It sounded like someone - or something - was stamping around in a terrible rage. The house grew hot and then very cold. There were blasts of icy air as if a fan had been switched on, then the lights started flashing."

Both Laura and Graham went upstairs to Danielle's room and as they opened the door they felt something rush out and *through* them. As they ran back downstairs in a panic the whole house started to vibrate. A terrific banging sound seemed to be coming from every room. Graham saw a silver flash darting down the stairs and could make out the outline of a man's head and shoulders.

Deciding it would be wise to all stay together, Laura and Graham moved the baby's cot into Laura's room, leaving the door slightly ajar. For a while everything was quiet, but gradually the light in the bedroom started to grow brighter and brighter until it glowed intense and white.

We grabbed the baby and ran...

"At this point we grabbed Danielle out of her cot and ran downstairs, out into the night. As we went the house seemed to light up like daylight."

With Laura and the baby safely installed at her parents' house nearby, Graham went back at 2.30am for Danielle's bottle, which had been forgotten in the rush to get out. "I can't believe I really did that. Looking back it was a stupid thing to do. When I pushed the door open there was a thick mist all through the house lit by a strange, bright white light which was growing more and more intense. I had just about enough. I grabbed the baby's bottle and ran," admitted Graham.

The house was let to new tenants and Graham, curious to know if they noticed anything odd there, called one day. "A chap came to the door. He had a young girl who I took to be his daughter, clinging to his legs. She had long blonde hair and was aged seven or eight. She smirked

Part of Clarence Road, East Cowes

at me but didn't speak. When I tried to warn the new tenant about our experiences there, he just looked at me like I was mad."

However, 18 months later, Laura, who now lives in Acorn Gardens, took a job in a local convenience store. One day, as she told the other staff about the haunted house, she had quite a shock when she realised one of them was the wife of the new tenant - and what's more - that the couple were childless. The woman told Laura that she and her husband had frequently seen the ghostly child, who appeared shortly after they moved in. Wearing an old-fashioned embroidered smock, and carrying a doll, she would sometimes try to get into their bed. The girl would stand at the front window waving if they came home late at night. She would sometimes even ride in their car with them! The little ghost liked to play with their answering machine and would also turn taps on, leaving the water running.

"I died in a cart accident"

This couple had tried to contact the spirit world using a Ouija board. The ghost's name was Lucy, they were told. Moving from letter to letter it spelled out: 'I am eel. I died in a cart accident in Rope Walk.' (Rope Walks were where hemp rope was twisted for ships' rigging. There was known to be one on the town's esplanade in the 19th century)

"Lucy apparently didn't like anyone else using 'her' room and was jealous of other children. A priest was subsequently called in to bless the house and the couple moved out after two years when they were expecting a baby. Another family live there now. I often wonder why the ghost showed herself to me that day I went round to warn the new people," said Graham.

Research shows that the house was built in 1949 on the site of an earlier dwelling wrecked by a wartime bomb. Parts of East Cowes - particularly the Clarence Road area - were heavily bombed during the Blitz, as the Luftwaffe targeted the nearby shipyard of J Samuel White and the aircraft factory of Saunders-Roe. On the night of 4 May 1942, the Island suffered its worst raid of the war, when some 150 Dornier bombers dropped 200 tons of high explosive and thousands of incendiary bombs, killing 70 people in Cowes and East Cowes and injuring many more.

One huge incendiary landed on the Castle Inn, one of the oldest pubs in the town, which stood at the corner of Clarence Road and Kings Road. It fell right through the building into the bar. Much to the relief of landlord Ernest Newberry, it failed to detonate immediately, giving time for the pub and neighbouring properties to be evacuated.

However a week later when the bomb went off, the resulting explosion completely demolished the pub and wrecked neighbouring properties, including the home of John Morey and his widowed sister Alice Deacon. This was one of a pair of late Victorian three-storey houses near to the Castle Inn. Although they escaped with their lives, many others were not so lucky. Mrs Deacon's son George was killed in the bombing and several other neighbours, including a pedestrian walking past the house, died in the Blitz.

So, as well as Lucy, the little spirit-child, who apparently met her end in a cart accident, who or what was responsible for Laura's terrifying experiences in that relatively modern house? Both Laura and Graham wonder if the resounding explosion which so unnerved them, was a ghostly echo from that violent past - not of the house - but of its site.

Author's note: In July 2000, Tigress Productions visited the Island to film this story for Channel Five TV. As Laura was being interviewed outside her former home, local psychic Margo Williams was able to make contact with Lucy's little spirit. Margo who experienced a great feeling of sadness while standing there, told the film crew that eight-year-old Lucy immediately recognised Danielle, now also aged eight, who was there with her mother.

"She said she was very sorry for frightening Danielle and meant her no harm, but had been jealous of her because she was loved and had toys, while she had nothing," Laura said. Margo who uses automatic writing when contacting spirits took down this message from Lucy: "Can you help me? My father was cruel and I was not allowed to play with children. My father beat me often. Please set me free. I died young. Never grew up. Can see a light. Will go towards it."

"I wanted to cry when I heard this," said Laura. "I am so happy that her little spirit has moved on, but it is so awful to think of the many long years she was earthbound; trapped there with her cruel and violent father. For his was the other presence we encountered in the house. The medium was not able to make contact with him or to help him leave. Unfortunately, it seems that **his** ghost may still be there…"

THE BOATYARD GHOST

Nearby in Clarence Boatyard, workers often hear odd noises coming from the corner of their workshop. "It isn't rats, it's the sound of someone, or something, rustling and moving about over by the door," said Eddie Richards, who runs the business with fellow boatbuilder Dave Hadden.

"We all hear it at odd times during the day and sometimes there is the feeling of a presence there too. Certainly if I come down here with my dog at night, he will never go in there."

One afternoon just before Christmas 1995, Eddie was working on the deck of a boat when he became aware of someone standing behind him and felt a gentle pressure on his arm. "I thought one of the lads wanted something, but when I turned there was no-one there. I don't know what haunts the place, but a workman was killed here some years ago when a lifeboat fell and crushed him," said Eddie.

Early in the New Year, the fax machine apparently went wrong. "We sent a fax to Souters at Cowes quoting a price for a job. But when it arrived at the other end it was complete gibberish. Souters rang to ask what we were playing at, because when the message came through it made no sense at all. They knew who had sent it because it was on E.D.J. headed business paper - the only trouble is we changed the firm's name some time ago and haven't used that paper for years - in fact there's none left anywhere.

"We couldn't understand what had happened. We even took the fax machine apart to see if there was any old headed paper jammed there somehow. There wasn't. But I think the ghost had been up to its tricks again," said Eddie.

OSBORNE'S PHANTOM CARRIAGE

Old East Cowes folk tell of a phantom horse-drawn carriage which, they say, can be heard galloping across what is now a golf course in the grounds of Queen Victoria's former home at Osborne House. But when Celia and Richard Flack moved to New Barn Road, which adjoins the estate, they knew nothing of this and indeed, would have laughed at such a tale.

Richard, a local businessman, was mystified when he actually heard the sound of two horses galloping through the grounds of the former Royal estate at 11.15pm on 8 February 1995. It was a still, clear night as he and Celia stood in their front garden; suddenly both heard noise like hoofbeats approaching at a gallop. These sounded as though two horses were coming towards them, from west to east, behind the fence to the Osborne grounds.

New Barn Road: where a phantom carriage was heard

"We could clearly hear them as they thundered passed us and then faded into the distance. Hearing horses out at that time of night was strange enough. But then we realised that no horse could have passed that way because of the dense undergrowth on the other side of the fence. It must have been the sound of ghost horses we heard that night. Since then we have been told about the phantom carriage. Perhaps there is something in that story after all," said Richard.

GHOST OF NEW BARN ROAD

Further along New Barn Road, a fifteen-year-old lad encountered a ghostly figure trudging towards Queen's Gate at about 10.30pm one night, some thirty years ago. Although he was prepared to tell me his story, he was reluctant for his name to be used, so I will call him Fred.

"I was riding my bike back from my uncle's house in Old Road towards York Avenue. It was a still night with no breeze; August or September it must have been. Although it was dark, there were a couple of street lamps, and at the side of the road ahead of me I could see a man's figure.

"I couldn't make out what he was wearing because he was between me and the street lamp so all I could see was his silhouette. I had no reason to notice him; he was just plodding at the side of the road, although, curiously, he made no sound.

"I pulled out to ride round him but as I drew level with him, he disappeared into thin air. Where he had been was icy cold. It was like riding into a blast of air from a freezer. I was still thoroughly chilled when I reached the main road, although I was pedalling like a goodun by this time," recalled Fred. "When I got home I didn't say much to anybody about what I had just seen because I don't really believe in ghosts. But I really can't explain what happened that night."

THE HAUNTED WHITE HART

A century ago, East Cowes was at the heart of the British Empire. With Queen Victoria in residence at Osborne House, the town, with its busy waterfront, was the entry point for visiting Royalty, ministers and diplomats. Whenever the monarch arrived on the Isle of Wight, she would alight at a specially constructed landing stage at Trinity Wharf, and drive in her carriage along Queens Road to Osborne.

The haunted White Hart Inn at East Cowes

Little evidence of her route survives today. Queens Road is now called Trinity Road, but on the corner overlooking the Red Funnel ferry terminal, the White Hart Inn still stands. It has resisted attempts at demolition or modernisation, apart from an episode in 1893, when the original inn dating back to 1748, was pulled down and rebuilt as a monument to late Victorian taste.

One ghost which haunts this pub is said to be that of a lady's maid from the Royal Estate, who had an affair with the landlord - although why her earthbound spirit should have chosen to linger in the back bar is unclear. However, she enjoys a degree of notoriety in death, with a brief appearance in the Campaign for Real Ale (CAMRA) Good Pub Guide!

Landlady Cherrill Barnes is certainly aware of the love-lorn ghost. "I have never seen her although on many occasions I have heard or sensed a presence. I am certain she is not alone and that there may be two other ghosts in different parts of the building.

"One night we had just closed and I was alone with Sandy, one of my regulars. I went to answer the phone and when I returned, Sandy said, 'I thought everyone had gone.'

"I assured her we were the only ones in the place, but Sandy insisted she had just seen someone walk right past me when I was on the phone."

One winter night after locking up, Cherrill settled down in front of the log burner with her cats. Suddenly the warm, cosy room felt icy cold. Both cats sat up as though watching something moving, then they raced out of the room.

Another strange event happened in 1995. Returning from an evening out, Cherrill found the pub in darkness. Her staff had cleared up and gone home, so she checked the premises were secure and went upstairs. "I was in bed with the cats, when I heard the sound of crockery rattling in the next room - like someone was making tea. Although I have bed and breakfast guests in from time to time, there was no one staying that night. I assumed one of my regulars must have arrived while I was out and that staff had forgotten to leave me a note. I knocked on the door, but the room was empty. I was alone in the pub."

Sometimes Cherrill hears a young woman's voice calling her name. The sound comes from the top of the staircase, but there's never anyone there. And the pub ghosts can often be a touch light-fingered. Objects frequently disappear, only to turn up again a couple of weeks later, but Cherrill is quite used to sharing the pub with ghosts by now.

In fact, she thought they had gone for good in 1999 after some building work. "I was quite upset. The place felt different without them. But I think they were just lying low, disturbed by the builders perhaps. I can feel they are back now - I have heard crockery rattling again in the dead of night, this time in the kitchen. Perhaps the ghostly maid is making tea again for her landlord lover."

Chapter Two

PHANTOMS OF PYLE STREET

THE DOWER HOUSE GHOST

When builders moved into a doctors' practice in Pyle Street, Newport, they disturbed more than they bargained for. And the work, which involved widening passageways, moving cupboards and making alterations to modernise the old building literally awakened the dead.

Jan Jarvis worked as a practice nurse at the surgery for almost five years, leaving in 1981. She recalls: "The builders were working on the first floor, widening the passageway and re-decorating the place. Every evening it was the nurse's job to tidy the doctor's room up there. One night, after surgery, I was just about to leave the room, having made sure everything was in its proper place, when I saw what looked like a small child in old-fashioned clothing flit past the door. It was a girl, aged about four or five years, who appeared to be wispy and white, not solid or substantial. She floated past me down the corridor, then disappeared. Her dress looked Victorian and very pretty - like party clothes. She made no sound. It all happened so quickly that I was quite taken aback."

When Jan told other staff of her extraordinary encounter, a receptionist who had worked in the building for years just smiled. "Oh yes, it's a ghost and she is well known. She has been seen quite a few times over the years in the same part of the building - even one of the doctors has met her in a first floor consulting room. We don't know who she is or what she is doing here, but she is quite harmless," the receptionist assured Jan.

Since then, The Dower House has undergone substantial renovation works and the little ghost has made herself scarce. One of the practice doctors, Richard Knight, never actually met her, but certainly doesn't dismiss the stories of hauntings. He admits that a series of loud bangs and crashes in that same room when he was alone in the building one evening, left him mystified and rather shaken. And he also confesses to a feeling of dread and unaccountable apprehension near a staircase on the ground floor. "I can't explain it but I get a really unpleasant sensation there. My hair stands on end and I feel quite uncomfortable."

A girl's ghost was seen here

The late Mary Watkin of Godshill, a retired nurse, confirmed that for years some staff had seen and spoken of the little ghost. She recalled that Richard Watson, who worked at The Dower House for a year as a young locum, complained of a presence and feeling of chill in one surgery. He flatly refused to see patients there after a picture on the wall jumped off a hook and fell to the floor as he watched.

Many nurses working in the building before it was renovated were reluctant to go upstairs after dark, maintaining there was a feeling that something was 'not right' in the little attic rooms.

One Saturday morning, a painter from East Cowes was decorating one of the surgeries when Mary went in with a mug of coffee for him. "I hope you haven't been too lonely in here all morning," she joked. "No, certainly not. I've had some fine company," said the workman. "I have had a little girl in here with me. She came to watch me stir my paint and she stood in the corner for ages just watching me work. A little thing she was in a pretty grey dress. She never spoke. She's gone now."

The Dower House has been used as a doctors' surgery, and latterly a health centre, for almost half a century. It was formerly two cottages, which were lodging or rooming houses. Situated in Pyle Street, one of the oldest - and most haunted areas of the town - it is surrounded by other properties of great age. Nearby Chantry House has a ghost known as Fred, while opposite, Orme House, the Apollo Theatre and the former Texas Homecare Centre, now BuyWise, have dark tales of their own. (Read about them in Ghost Books I and II and the Newport Ghostwalk).

The haunted Dower House, Newport

A KIND OF SOUL

In 1835 there were no fewer than 35 boot and shoemakers in Newport, quite a feat for a town with less than 3,000 inhabitants! Nowadays, just a handful of shoe shops and cobblers remain. However, at the While U Wait Service at 70 Pyle Street, there among the shoes awaiting repair, the racks of heels, soles and lasts, lingers a very different kind of soul....

The ghost here manifests in a variety of ways. Once, as an exquisite perfume, so fragrant that employee Ruth Bennett said she had never smelled anything so beautiful in her life.

"It was a wonderful smell and quite unexpected. I was there alone; the shop was closed and I was in an area under the stairs when I noticed this amazing perfume. It was so very localised that I could literally walk in and out of the fragrance. Sadly I have never smelled it since. If you could bottle that perfume, it would really sell."

On another occasion, Ruth was working at a sewing machine, stitching a pair of shoes, when she felt someone behind her. "I put my hand out and touched what felt like a heavy cotton cloth. But when I turned to see who it was, the shop was empty; no-one was there."

Perhaps the apparition seen by proprietor Lynn Holdaway in that area under the stairs was responsible for the fragrance which Ruth so enjoyed. "She was a big woman, quite tall, wearing a long, dark grey flannel dress, a white apron and something white on her head. I thought at first it was a real person, she looked so solid. She was reaching up to a shelf and appeared to be putting something on it. It gave me such a shock that I backed away, and when I looked again she had gone.

"I have only seen her that one time but we often feel her presence and we all call her Ethel. When things go missing here, as they often do, Ethel gets the blame. You can put tools down beside you and a moment later they have vanished. They generally turn up again, three weeks later, in a stupid place.

"The shop and workrooms are always cold. Even in the middle of summer we can never get them warm. We often feel her presence when working at the sewing machine. It's like having someone looking over your shoulder. At other times you can see a shadow moving about in the rooms behind the shop and through a door.

Once Ruth saw a small tin of paint rise into the air and fly across the room. The work of an unseen hand. But whose hand? In its time

Number 70 Pyle Street has been many things; for years the town's housewives bought their meat there from butcher, Stanley Stevens, while early in the last century the premises belonged to Isaac Hayward, baker. In 1879 the shop was owned by William Downer - who was one of those 35 shoemakers in the town! Now the wheel has turned full circle. Perhaps the ghostly Ethel was employed then and is still trying to help repair shoes in the 21st century.

THE CHRISTMAS SPIRIT

Meanwhile, in Scarrots Lane which is linked to Pyle Street through Gray's Walk, a ghost full of seasonal spirit left an ancient faded message at a Newport hairdressing and beauty salon, wishing everyone "Merry Christmas"

As unlikely as it sounds, that's the conclusion hairdresser Jason Catania and his former business partner, Lisa, arrived at in December 1998. Early one morning they were getting ready to open their salon, Diva, when Lisa came running downstairs clutching a faded yellowing piece of parchment with the words *MERRY CHRISTMAS* printed in an old-fashioned script. "She looked quite pale and blurted out, 'I think I've just seen a ghost'."

A 'Seasonal Spirit' haunts here

Jason continued, "Lisa was in quite a state after seeing a vague figure in the beauty salon upstairs which had apparently left this message for us. I really thought she was having me on and had made it up, but since then, a whole lot of other things have happened here that I can't explain.

"There is often the smell of burning toast wafting about upstairs, although there's no cooker or toaster there. Wheeled chairs move by themselves across the room and there is sometimes a feeling that someone or some invisible presence is there with you."

Diva, which opened in October 1998, is in a quaint little flagstoned courtyard off Scarrots Lane, in premises previously used as plumber's yard. A century earlier, Victorian stables and a hayloft occupied the site, and when the area was excavated for the courtyard, the complete skeleton of a horse was found there.

Jason has no idea who, or what, appears to be haunting Diva. But whatever it is confines itself to that upstairs room, now a storeroom, and doesn't bother staff or clients. Save for the smell of burnt toast and the odd Christmas greeting, you hardly know it's there.

SPIRITS AT THE OLD BROWN JUG

For over a century, the Brown Jug served the people of Pyle Street. Many pubs offered a bottle and jug service and the Brown Jug took its name from one of the containers used to fetch the beer. It closed as a public house in the early 1970s, becoming Newport's Liberal Club instead. Several distinct presences have been seen, heard and felt there, and leading local councillors are among those who were reluctant to work alone in the first floor offices after dark.

Georgina Viney of Manor Crescent, Newport, worked there first as a cleaner; later she did bar work, before taking over as steward. Her experiences at the old pub therefore span several years.

"I really thought what was happening there would drive me mad," said Georgina. "It was silly little things at first. I would lock up securely at night, but the next morning when I arrived, the door would be unlocked. One day I put my heavy set of keys down on the bar counter, but when I turned to pick them up they weren't there. My husband, George, and I searched everywhere, including the cellar and the garden; we even looked in the shed outside. Those keys were nowhere to be found. We had to have every lock in the place changed. Then two days later they turned up again - out in the shed.

"Often when George went out to the toilet, the door would open on its own for him. After a while he got so used to it he would just call out 'Thank you, Fred' and when he was playing the club's fruit machine he would say 'Come on Fred, let's have that jackpot!' What's more, it would sometimes happen.

"When I left, usually around midnight or 1am, I would turn off all the lights and lock the door. But when I looked back, the lights would be on

The old Brown Jug stood on the left, where High Street meets Carisbrooke Road

again. In one of the rooms between the bar and kitchen, there was always a feeling of cold - but curiously, you would only feel it from the knees down.

"I became so concerned that I called in a local clergyman, Reverend James Buckett. He told me he thought we had a poltergeist in the place. So George did some research into the history of the Brown Jug. He discovered that in 1878-9 it was run by Sarah Reason whose husband, Thomas, had owned a brewery at Coppins Bridge since the 1830s.

"Infant mortality was common in those days and sadly the couple lost three of their children. One drowned; another succumbed to illness; the third was run over by a cart. This actually made sense to us, as the hauntings were rather childish. Sometimes we could hear a little giggle and I would feel someone tapping me on the shoulder, but whenever I turned round there was never anyone there," said Georgina.

Three Ghosts on a Stair

Jo Mayes, who lives in nearby New Street, worked behind the bar at the Liberal Club for 15 years; for part of that time she was also a Club Steward. She recalled, "Whatever haunted the ground floor and cellars was childish and mischievous, but upstairs it was something different altogether.

"Downstairs there were ghostly children. A psychic member actually saw three of them sitting on the stairs one day. They seemed to enjoy playing harmless pranks in the bar and cellars. Beer taps were turned on and off, glasses and furniture were moved. If any children came into the club, the spirit children would become more active. Keys would frequently go missing; people would put them down in the bar and they would turn up later in the garden. One December I arrived at work to find every Christmas decoration had been taken down and piled in the centre of the floor, while the tree was tipped on its side."

The ghost-children never seemed to go upstairs, however. That was the preserve of two dark-clad phantoms. One, known as 'the lady in black', was seen coming through the back door and gliding silently up the rear staircase. Another member of staff was always pleased when this particular spirit was around. "The lady brings me good luck," she insisted.

A busy estate agent's office has now replaced the former pub

Other people who regularly used the building were not so happy. Offices on the first floor became the headquarters of the Island's Liberal Association. Isle of Wight Council Leader, Shirley Smart, recalls, "I would often work there late at night, sometimes into the early hours, but never on my own. Few of us were brave enough to remain there alone after dark. There was a definite presence, but only at night. Several times I saw the outline of a man in black, wearing a long dark cape or cloak."

Retired midwife and former IW Councillor, Val Taylor of Ventnor, also glimpsed the figure in those first floor offices. "The place was absolutely fine during the day. Downstairs the spirit-children would be around. They were just mischievous and we would sometimes hear a little ghostly giggle. It was so funny and rather charming. Upstairs however, the atmosphere changed as darkness fell. It was a horrible feeling, oppressive and quite unpleasant. Both Shirley and I could feel it late at night. We would not stay there alone. You were aware of "something" watching you. It was very uncomfortable," said Val.

Retired JP and former Chairman of the Isle of Wight County Council, Bernard Pratt, confirms, "There was talk of a presence there. I never experienced anything myself, but I know that Val and others would never work late in the office upstairs on their own."

Like the Brown Jug before it, Newport Liberal Club, which closed in 1996, is now just a memory. The building has since been extensively modernised. Marvins Estate Agency, run by Mark Roberts, a partner in Marvins, now occupies the ground floor. Local architect, Harry Wheeler, has an office and apartment above. Mention of those ghostly goings-on in the old pub was met with amusement and frank incredulity by both. "All is now quiet. The spirits have definitely departed," they confirmed.

Chapter Three

VILLAGE WRAITHS

CHARLIE THE POLTERGEIST 'CHIPPY'

After spending years at a Whitwell farmhouse, a poltergeist went on its travels, accompanying a visitor back to her home in Stratford-upon-Avon. Charlie, as he was known by Cliff and Betty Matthews of Moorhills, disappeared from their home and lives, the very day that a former occupant of the house arrived unannounced.

Cliff, who for years ran a well-known timber and fencing business at Fishbourne, bought Moorhills, a 17th century longhouse built of stone, for his retirement in 1971. He encountered the poltergeist a number of times, growing quite accustomed to its pranks, which usually involved tools in the nearby timber workshop and sawmill.

"Charlie was here when we took over the house although we were not really aware of him until several months later when tools started to move around or disappear. However we never really minded his presence as it was always friendly, if a bit mischievous."

One day Cliff started to replace floorboards suffering from dry rot. When he finished that night, he left the carpet rolled up with a heavy bookcase laid across it. But when he returned the following day, he couldn't start work because his saw had disappeared.

"We hunted everywhere for that saw. In the end I had to go to the farm to find an old one to finish the job. Several days later we unrolled the carpet, and there, three turns from the centre, was the missing saw, its blade split into two pieces. It was quite bizarre," said Cliff.

Tools featured in another odd episode when one of Cliff's workers, Bill Main, complained that someone had cracked the mouth of his steel plane. "No-one owned up to doing it, so I got a piece of glass paper and polished it to see if it was a proper crack or just a scratch. That crack was big enough to put a fingernail in," Cliff insisted.

"Three months later I found Bill standing with his plane in hand, looking puzzled. It was easy to recognise because it had some old paint spots on it. Although it was the same plane, the crack had completely disappeared. Bill had carried on using the plane because it still worked, despite the damage."

Cliff and Betty Matthews at haunted Moorhills, Whitwell

It seems that Charlie found Bill an easy target for his pranks, sometimes moving his saw from one end of the workshop to the other, and when he put tools down, he would often turn round to find them hanging neatly on the wall.

One day a woman named Win turned up asking if she could look around. She explained to Cliff and Betty that she had lived at Moorhills as a child. She was interested in seeing what they had done to her old house and in reviving some memories. Her visit certainly did more than revive old memories for Charlie the ghost. He promptly attached himself to her, travelling back to her mainland home where he has now installed himself in her hall. "We didn't notice that Charlie had actually gone for several months, but after a while I realised that nothing more had happened and wondered if Win had somehow taken him away with her," said Cliff.

"About a year later, Win came for another visit with her sister and their respective husbands. They all stayed for supper and we had an enjoyable evening together. I took Win to see a puppet theatre I had built for my grandchildren in one of the barns and while we were by ourselves I took the opportunity ask about Charlie. Rather embarrassed I said, 'We had a poltergeist here and now it's gone. I think you took it away with you.'

"Yes I know I did," Win laughed. "I can tell you where it is now. It is on my landing in our home in Stratford and it keeps unscrewing lamp shades there."

With that, the subject was closed. Win always remembers to send a Christmas card and note to which she adds, "I have still got Charlie". On a visit to Moorhills in April 2000, she reported that the poltergeist was still up to its tricks and had just caused chaos by hiding her spectacles in a piano stool lid.

A CHARMING STONE COTTAGE.......

A charming stone cottage in Whitwell High Street appeared at first sight to be the ideal home for Beth Carter, her baby daughter Faith, and fiance John.

When Beth and John rented their cottage in June 1992, they knew nothing of its history, but have since learned that it was built almost 300 years ago. However, as quaint and peaceful as their new home appeared, things were not what they seemed for Beth soon discovered the cottage was haunted.

The first manifestations she noticed were light footsteps coming from the baby's bedroom overhead. Little Faith, who was only three months old, certainly wasn't responsible for the noises and there were no pets in the house either. "They sounded as though a young child was running about upstairs. It usually happened at about 5pm, and although I would rush upstairs immediately, I could never find out what or who was causing them," said Beth.

As a chef, John often worked at night, so Beth was alone in the cottage with the baby. And while he was out, almost every evening between 9pm and 9.05pm, she would hear the little side gate open; heavy footsteps would walk down the path; then the back door would start to rattle. "Sometimes I would glimpse a shadowy figure moving past the window, but mostly there was nothing there at all. This went on for several months. I actually grew quite used to it and tried to persuade myself I was imagining things."

On 15 April 1993, John's parents were visiting the cottage when the nightly noises started. "The gate slammed loudly and we all heard what sounded like the heavy footsteps of a man wearing work boots trudging up to the back door. As we all looked towards the door it suddenly flew open … but no one came in.

"Soon afterwards John's parents went home. I think his dad was scared stiff by what had happened. He certainly never came over to baby-sit again," Beth said. Her brother Paul, who also admitted feeling uneasy there, refused to babysit too. "It is a very strange place. There is something very uncomfortable there," he acknowledged.

The cottage was also plagued by smells, which had no obvious origin. One particularly strong odour became a standing joke with the couple's friends who nicknamed their home the 'smoky bacon' house.

Beth explained, "The smell of smoked bacon was overpowering sometimes. It was a very localised phenomenon, which usually occurred at the top of the stairs. The strange thing was that you could walk into the smell and then out again the other side. Sometimes it was so strong, it was as if I had put my face up against a side of smoked bacon."

Beth first noticed this aroma three months after she moved to the cottage, but it was not until February 1993 that John caught his first whiff of it. "Until then he thought it was just a laugh and said I was imagining things. But on this particular evening I noticed it first just at the top of the stairs and it was so strong that I called to John to come and see if he could smell anything.

"He is a 16 stone, 6ft 2in tall rugby player who certainly doesn't scare easily. But that night when he came downstairs his face was completely white and waxen; his beard and hair were standing on end. 'My God. You are right. I CAN smell it', he said."

A dank, rotting stench

The cottage's other odour, which a number of people had noticed, was a dank, rotting stench which sometimes lingered near the front door and in part of the lounge. This malodorous, pervasive smell often appeared between 11pm and midnight, even in the summer.

"We had the drains checked, the floorboards up, and even had the chimney swept to see if something had died and was rotting there. We found nothing. Strangely though, when the light was switched on, the putrid mildewy odour would rapidly dissipate. It was a very cold house - abnormally cold - even in the middle of July we would light the fire to try to warm the place up.

"It was always freezing cold even with the storage heaters going full

High Street, Whitwell, at the turn of the last century

blast. Although it appeared very homely and lived-in, especially with a nice log fire, guests did not stay long. They would huddle over the fire commenting how cold it was. But it was not just draughty there. It was a frigid, bone-chilling cold."

Beth had a particular dread of the lounge although there was no rational explanation for this. "I was very uneasy and became terrified of going in there at night. If I had to go downstairs to the bathroom in the early hours I would turn all the lights on and shut the door quickly. I was scared of what I might see in there."

One night Beth woke at 1.45am with a strong premonition that something was about to happen. Suddenly there was a loud crash from downstairs. She and John rushed down, to find that a huge picture which hung on the stairwell had fallen off the wall, down seven stairs, to land six feet across the kitchen floor resting against the tumble dryer. "The picture string had not broken and the nail it had hung from was still firmly embedded in the wall. It was quite impossible for it to have fallen naturally because when we found it, the picture was actually standing upright, the right way up, facing out as if it had been deliberately placed there," recalled Beth.

Often, small objects such as keys, pens and jewellery, would completely vanish, reappearing only after an exhaustive search - back in their original place.

"It was not a happy house or a very lucky one," said Beth. "I was on edge there all the time. I would use any excuse to get away. I didn't realise until we moved out just how much time I spent at my parents' house or just driving around so that I did not have to go home when John was out working. When we lived there we seemed to argue all the time. The cottage had a really bad atmosphere. The baby was restless and unsettled and I sometimes experienced an overwhelming feeling of loneliness and despair there."

After just 18 months at Whitwell, the family moved out. The cottage was put up for sale, but remained on the market more than two years before new owners moved in. Since then the property has been for sale several times.

"We were just glad to get away," said Beth. "We never discovered any reason for the strange happenings in that place. I only hope the present occupants have better luck there than we did."

SPIRITS OF SHORWELL

Late spring is a good time to visit the village of Shorwell. At twilight the distinctive scent of the wild garlic which covers the banks of the steep shute can be overpowering. Its pungent odour may frighten vampires, but it doesn't deter the local ghosts.

A leafy, tree-lined road winds down towards Shorwell, under a little rustic wooden bridge and past historic Northcourt Manor. At the foot of Shorwell Shute stands a row of quaintly picturesque thatched stone cottages. Once these tiny dwellings, built in 1720, served as farm labourers' cottages for the nearby manor. Today, their rural origins are a faint memory. But in one of the cottages, the ghost of a long-dead villager lives on.

When Jeremy Brown and his catering business partner, Gary Barton, moved into their cottage, they had no idea that it was haunted by a ghost which regarded the spare room as hers. "We hardly liked to use it - we

Picturesque thatched cottages at the foot of Shorwell Shute

felt that we were intruding," said Jeremy.

Their ghost may only have used candles or oil lamps in her day, but she, for it was a female presence, quickly became accustomed to the novelty and convenience of electric lights, continually switching them on in 'her' room. She also had an uncomfortable habit of leaving the front door wide open when Jeremy and Gary had locked and latched it.

"Many times we came home late at night to find the porch door shut and the front door wide open. It was simply impossible for it to have blown open. Many times too, we were in the sitting room when the door to the kitchen unlatched and opened all by itself."

Despite this, they quite enjoyed sharing their home with the ghost. "We never saw her, but think she was a kindly person. Although she left doors open, she did help to keep the place warm. In the winter, despite the front door being wide open, the house would feel as warm as toast, except for 'her' room, which was always freezing cold," added Gary.

Further down the road, almost opposite the church, stands another cottage with a resident ghost. The family who have lived here for over 25 years, are reluctant to talk about their spirit in case by doing so, they empower it to grow stronger and more active. The old stone cottage, once part of the Northcourt estate, is haunted by the sound of footsteps and what Di, the lady of the house, describes as "benign bumps".

St Mary's Church at Carisbrooke, where a black-gowned ghost was seen

Chapter Four

GHOSTS WALK THERE

WILHEMINA AT THE WAVERLEY

Although situated near the centre of the Island, the Waverley Hotel at Carisbrooke, still has a tang of the sea about it. Standing at the crossroads at the top of the High Street, it resembles a Victorian railway hotel - minus the railway.

Now a Grade II listed building, it is a classic 19th century commercial hotel, built in 1852 on the instructions of Captain Wakeham, a sailing ship skipper, and supposedly named after one of his favourite shipping lines.

The hotel ghost, who has been dubbed Wilhemina, made herself known to Terrie and Peter Potter shortly after they took over the Waverley in 1994. Her mischievous, child-like pranks lead the couple to believe that Wilhemina could be the spirit of a licensee's young daughter who, according to an elderly village resident, tragically died of meningitis there some 70 years earlier.

"We feel her all over the building, from the cellars to the top of the house. She is a friendly and playful little ghost who seems to delight in mischief," smiled Terrie. "She seems to enjoy moving or hiding things and I am sure she occasionally goes through my jewellery. Things disappear, only to turn up days or weeks later in the strangest places."

Sometimes when the bar is busy, staff find the gas tap which pumps all the beer from the old cellar has mysteriously been turned off. It is quite impossible for this to happen accidentally. Meanwhile down in that cellar, a mallet used for knocking taps into the kegs and barrels frequently goes missing. "You can put it down beside you, turn around, and it will vanish, turning up later in the most unlikely place," said Terrie.

Staff past and present have smelled the strong scent of old lavender in the kitchens downstairs, and occasionally early of a morning (always on a Wednesday) the smell of warm toasting bread wafts around the pub for no apparent reason. A barmaid who slept in the hotel overnight heard the distinctive sound of an old fashioned typewriter being used in the empty room next to her bedroom, during the early hours.

Built in 1852, the Waverley Hotel is home to a ghost called Wilhemina

Terrie came downstairs one morning to discover all the pool cues were arranged in a pattern on the floor. Later, while she was standing behind the bar, she felt the lightest of touches, as though a small hand had brushed through her hair from the back of her neck forwards.

Recently, a visitor to the Waverley sporting a very short 'grade one' haircut, had a similar experience, and confided to Terrie that he had felt invisible hands touching his head. "Wilhemina was clearly intrigued to see such a close cut and wanted to stroke it," she said.

"Sometimes we hear the front door open and close by itself, but there is never anybody there. This even happened very late one night when we had locked all the doors, washed up and were sitting playing cards at 2am. The door opened, then closed, and we heard the sound of footsteps on the stairs," Terrie recalled.

Only once so far, has Wilhemina shown herself. One night in May 1995, Mike, a musician who had been playing in a band at the Waverley left the hotel at about 11.45pm. As he was loading equipment into his car, he felt a compulsion to look up at a square glass tower at the top of the hotel, known as the watchtower. There, framed in the glass for an instant, was the figure of a young woman or girl with blonde hair - he couldn't see clearly.

The Waverley in the year 2000 remains a popular 'local' for the people of Carisbrooke

But whatever it was Mike glimpsed that night must have been standing in mid-air because there is no floor. The glass sides of the watchtower are at least 15ft from first floor landing....

LADY IN BLACK

It was a beautiful, hot August day when the Shingler family got off the bus at Carisbrooke. It was their first visit to the Isle of Wight and the sleepy village seemed far removed from their home town of Wolverhampton. The year was 1956. Mr and Mrs Shingler with their daughter, Stephanie, decided to take a look in the old Norman church of St Mary's.

Stephanie recalls, "It was very dark inside, quite gloomy and cool. All of the windows as far as I can remember were stained glass in those days. We paused at the back of the church for a moment then began to walk up the aisle.

"As we did so, a lady who was kneeling in front of the altar got up and moved towards us, making no sound as she walked. She was wearing a long black gown and we were struck by her costume and the Tudor-style headdress with rows of black beads hanging down. Her face

St Mary's Church, Carisbrooke, seen from the air

which we glimpsed through the beads appeared very white - almost like marble.

"We stood aside for her to pass and Mum squeezed my hand. The lady did not look at us, and made no sound as she went by. She went to the back of the church......then vanished. None of us spoke until we were outside in the warm sunshine again. Then we realised we had just seen a ghost."

Interestingly, the church interior was renovated shortly afterwards and the stained glass was replaced with clear windows, so the church is now much lighter.

The Shinglers have been back a number of times since then but have had no further sightings of the black-garbed figure. However, Mrs Shingler found herself drawn to an ancient tomb at the rear of the church, belonging to a mother and her baby who were buried together.

"A feeling of coldness and melancholy envelop me when I stand there," she sighed. "I feel sure there is a connection to the ghost of that unhappy woman in black."

A TRAGIC PRINCESS

For more than nine centuries Carisbrooke Castle has played a major part in the Island's history. During its turbulent past it has stood firm against attack, a symbol of strength, a refuge for the townspeople of Newport when invaders threatened. The home of Isle of Wight Governors, it was once even the prison of a king and two of his children.

A year after King Charles I was executed in London, in August 1650 Princess Elizabeth and her brother, Henry, Duke of Gloucester, were brought as prisoners to the castle from which their father failed to escape.

Elizabeth, a delicate but intensely gifted child, apparently suffered from rickets which afflicted her legs. She was there but a short time, for she developed a chill after being caught in the rain on the castle bowling green. Complications developed and she died on 8 September 1650, shortly before her fifteenth birthday. Her embalmed body was brought from the castle and interred in a lead coffin in front of the altar in

The Governor's House at Carisbrooke Castle where the young princess was incarcerated

Newport's twelfth century St Thomas of Canterbury church. When the old building was demolished, Queen Victoria commissioned a white marble effigy of the captive princess, her face resting on the Bible which had been her father's parting gift, to grace the new building.

Her brother remained in captivity at Carisbrooke until 1653 when he was set free and allowed to join his brother Charles in France. Before her sudden and tragically early demise, it is reported that Cromwell was

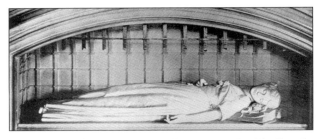

Memorial to the tragic princess in Newport Parish Church

making plans to have the young princess set to work and apprenticed to a Newport button maker.

Could it have been her sad spirit which one day attached itself to a psychic visitor when she looked around the room in which the young princess died? A member of staff at Carisbrooke Castle Museum was startled when a woman came downstairs from that bedroom and told her, "There is a presence with me. She wanted to be carried downstairs. I have taken her outside and she is happy now." With that, the woman left the castle.

A GIN FOR THE GHOST

The Sun Inn at Hulverstone is a traditional country pub. A delightful old-fashioned thatched inn with flagstone floors, a huge open fireplace and log fires in the winter. Hulverstone, between Brook and Mottistone is a tiny hamlet, and with no shop, the pub is the focus of life there. Such pubs are often haunted and the Sun Inn upholds this tradition with enthusiasm.

Recently, its fate hung in the balance after the little pub was closed and converted into a private dwelling. Dismayed at this, the local community campaigned for its reinstatement and after a three-day planning appeal, the inspector ruled in their favour. The Sun Inn now has a new owner, Bruce Loneragan, and delighted residents have their local back again. What the resident ghost thinks of all this has yet to be seen.

Back in 1994, Pam White and Ray Steele who took over as licensees of the 500-year-old former alehouse quickly grew accustomed to the ghost's antics. Bizarre happenings with no explanation, they started at dead of night with the creaking of door handles.

One day Ray noticed movement in the empty bar and there, reflected in the glass of a picture opposite, he saw a man's face looking out at him. "It certainly wasn't my face reflected in there. It was a complete stranger", Ray said. Clearing up one night when the bar was closed, he looked up to see the apparition of an oldish man wearing grey, baggy trousers, and a maroon woollen v-neck pullover, standing there.

One morning Pam came downstairs to find knives and forks which she had carefully wrapped in paper napkins ready for the next day, had all been unwrapped and the napkins had vanished. The same thing happened the next morning, but this time the cutlery had been laid out by unseen hands, with the knives and forks crossed.

Two friends staying at the pub decided to sleep downstairs in front of the fire one cold winter night. However they didn't get much rest, for their sleep was disturbed by the sound of someone in the room, who was rolling marbles across the flagstone floor.

As happens in many such hauntings, small objects would often disappear for days or months on end. Pam's purse and Ray's car keys both went missing at the same time. Everyone hunted high and low for them; three months later the purse appeared, complete with money, in the middle of the bedroom floor. The keys turned up a month after that in another bedroom.

The ghost's light-fingered tendencies caused a panic one night when the bar takings went missing. Ray had put all the cash from the till in a money bag ready for banking. "We searched for hours for that bag; we almost took the place apart. Finally we appealed to the ghost to put it back - if it was responsible. Lo and behold, shortly afterwards, the bag appeared on the stone floor behind the bar, where we could not miss it."

A brass hunting horn mouthpiece vanished from the bar wall, only to turn up on top of the fridge three months later. Occasionally hunting pictures fell off the walls - for no reason - and the brass poker hanging by the chimney would start to swing violently when the fire needed attention.

Customers occasionally asked if the pub was haunted. One lady was convinced there was 'something' haunting the toilets. Although the rest of the inn felt warm and friendly, Pam was the first to agree that this part was not nice.

"The toilet was always extremely chilly and locals joked that it was the coldest loo in the West Wight," she laughed. "Whatever was here became active for a while every two or three months and then went quiet again. But it's a friendly ghost and I rather liked having it around," admitted Pam. "I always said goodnight to it when I went up to bed."

Drinks would disappear

As a pub ghost it liked the odd tipple and occasionally helped itself to a drink. "It sounds crazy but drinks did disappear," said Ray, who did not believe in ghosts until he moved to that haunted inn. "Several times I served customers with drinks, put a pint of beer on the counter, and had the customer ask again for the beer. At first we thought it was people trying to get a free drink, but it happened too many times. We would always find the missing pint later, usually in a quite incongruous place."

Shortly after Pam and Ray installed a new itemised automatic till; a £1 price ticket fell off an optic onto the floor. Unsure where it belonged, Ray and the barman decided it had probably come from the gin. Suddenly, just as they were about to replace it, the till rang up £1 for a measure of gin... all by itself.

Pam, who had heard all this from the kitchen, said she would have the gin that had been rung up. She poured one, added ice to it and put it down on the bar. It vanished, never to be seen again!

Chapter Five

SPIRITS OF COWES

GHOST DOG AT MARINE COURT

The little brown and white Jack Russell appeared just as Barry Reed was about to lock up for the night. It was June 1998 and Barry, who has worked as manager of the Isle of Wight Model Railway Exhibition on Cowes Parade since 1994, was turning off all the train layouts and exhibits when he saw the scruffy little dog sitting at the end of one of the walkways.

"This is all I need!" he muttered to himself, as he went to chase the animal out. But the dog had disappeared and Barry spent the next hour hunting high and low for it. He even pulled up the wooden entrance ramp in case the Jack Russell was hiding there. He found nothing. The place was silent and deserted; the dog was nowhere to be found. By now it was getting on for 7pm so Barry locked up and went home - still puzzled. Perhaps it had somehow squeezed through somewhere and escaped. He half expected to find it still there next morning when he arrived for work, but there was no sign of the little intruder.

The old Royal Marine Hotel on Cowes Parade in the 1920s

Many crowned heads of Europe stayed at the haunted hotel

A year later Barry had all but forgotten the incident. He was opening the exhibition and shop at 10am, switching the lighting on and starting the trains running, when he saw the little dog again. It was sitting between the shop and layout room. It made no sound, but just vanished.

"I combed that building although there was absolutely no way the dog could have got out. I even rang Patrick, my boss, to tell him there was a dog loose in here and I couldn't find it. I know what I saw; I didn't imagine the dog. It looked real enough, but made no sound. It was June on both occasions I saw it, so I'll be keeping a special watch every year from now on," said Barry.

In fact, the dog made its next appearance in mid-May 2000 and Barry was not the one to see it. This time it was the turn of 17-year-old David Smart, who helps Barry on Saturdays, to both see and hear the animal. Barry explained, "It was about 5.30pm on Saturday 20 May, when I came into the shop and found David shaking in his chair. Although there were no visitors, he had heard scratching noises coming from the lobby area between the shop and layout room. At first he thought it was me messing about, but then he saw the dog!"

The room where the little dog appeared was formerly part of the extensive kitchens at the 200-year-old Drover's Marine Hotel, later renamed the Royal Marine Hotel, one of the most prestigious in Cowes. Its guest book, now at Cowes Maritime Museum, reads like a Who's

Who of European Royalty. In its hey-day it was *the* place in Cowes to stay for the summer yachting season.

Now known as Marine Court and converted into apartments and offices, its top storey removed, the once impressive building still retains traces of earlier elegance. But the mystery remains, who owned the little ghost-dog and why does it appear in the early summer?

THE GRANTHAM GHOST

The Grantham Hotel in Queen's Road at Cowes, was one of the best known hotels in the town. Built in 1837, the year Queen Victoria came to the throne, it was the home of George Robert Stephenson, nephew of the inventor of 'The Rocket', and local benefactor, who gave the nearby Green (later named Princes Green) to the people of Cowes. Just a few hundred yards from the Royal Yacht Squadron, the seafront hotel which opened in 1948, was run by the Peacock family until it was demolished in the early 1990s, to make way for a block of luxury apartments.

Tony Gower of Lark Rise, Carisbrooke, has fond memories of the old hotel, for between 1983-1984 it became a second home for him while he set up a business on the Island. "It was a strange old building with rooms at different levels, but I was always made very welcome there. My favourite was room five, which stood on its own right at the top of the hotel under the eaves, overlooking the sea. A feature of the room was the big marble fireplace with a mirror above. On the table was a large glass ash tray which I kept my loose change in, as I am not a smoker.

"One morning I woke suddenly at 5.30am, in time to see that heavy ashtray fly at speed through the air some 12-14ft across the room, crashing to the floor with such force that it broke into a thousand pieces sending glass and coins everywhere. It was as if it had been thrown violently. I didn't get any sleep after that!"

At breakfast Tony asked if the hotel was haunted. "Certainly not" he was told. But he has since discovered that other guests reported odd happenings there, especially on the staircase leading to room five.

Tony runs a factory in Cowes, and Eileen, a member of his staff who once worked at the Grantham, told him, "All sorts of strange things happened in that place. There were various 'cold spots' and some mornings we would come in to find things had been moved around in the night. You were certainly not the first guest to complain that room five was haunted."

Once one of the best known hotels in Cowes, the haunted Grantham Hotel was demolished in the 1990s to make way for luxury appartments

Jill Chapman (formerly Jill Wyatt and a member of the Peacock family), who now lives at Park Road, Wootton, remembers Tony well, for they still exchange cards at Christmas. "As to ghosts at the hotel, I never saw or heard anything myself," she said. But after a moment's thought added, "For a very long time an elderly lady, Miss Aubrey, lived with us between Easter and November each year.

"Miss Aubrey sometimes remarked that she could hear a ghost moving about in her room. This ghost would open her window in the night. We thought she was imagining things and never took her seriously though. Perhaps the Grantham really was haunted after all!"

A POWER HUNGRY SPIRIT?

Do ghosts somehow tap into energy sources in order to materialise? An entity which haunted a house at Arctic Road, Cowes, managed to run up an electricity bill of more than £800. After just five months at the end of terrace house, Sharon McGrath was astonished to receive an astronomical bill for £874, which she believes the ghost was responsible for. Actually, she was expecting a high gas bill, because whatever haunted the little house was continually playing with the gas taps on the cooker and would often turn all four on together.

The first inkling Sharon and her boyfriend had that all was not as it seemed at the house came shortly after they moved in. A friend's two young daughters who stayed the night in the spare room complained that they had felt an extra foot in the bed. Naturally Sharon paid no heed to such a ridiculous tale.

Two days later she smelled gas and hurrying into the kitchen found all four rings were switched on, but not alight. Over the next five months this happened countless times and Sharon became so concerned that she started leaving the kitchen window open. Bath and basin taps in the bathroom, directly overhead, would also be turned full on and Sharon would hear footsteps and what sounded like a two-way radio coming from the empty bathroom.

Her dogs would often sit and bark at an old chair in the front room, and none of her pets, including the cats, would ever sit in it. Fearful of what was going on in the otherwise normal house, Sharon called on the nearby Spiritualist Church for help. "A few of the members came round and held a prayer meeting at the house one evening. While they were there, the gas came on in the kitchen and they managed to make contact with my ghost.

"The Spiritualists told me that a Mr Carpenter had died in the house many years before. People at the time thought he had committed suicide, but his ghost told the Spiritualists it had been an accident. He did not comprehend that he was dead and his spirit continued to occupy his old house.

"After they left we asked neighbours about this. One elderly woman recalled that about seventy years earlier, a couple named Carpenter had lived there. Apparently, after the wife died, the man was unable to look after himself properly and had been found gassed in the kitchen."

Despite the visit from the Spiritualists, the ghost continued to roam the house switching lights, gas and water taps on. He even entertained on a piano, which had been left in the former basement kitchen. This room, which was directly below the present kitchen and bathroom, was always uncommonly cold.

Curiously, during her five months at Arctic Road, Sharon did not receive any bills for services such as gas, electricity and telephone. "At first it was nice, but I started to worry. I asked the postman what had happened to them, but he got a bit offended and said he was putting all my post through the letter-box."

When Sharon discovered her telephone directories were being

The town of Cowes from the air showing part of Arctic Road, where a ghost ran up a huge electricity bill for an unfortunate woman

shredded into tiny pieces, her suspicion naturally turned to the dogs. However, when the replacement books - and other items of post - were found ripped into shreds in a locked room, she knew they could not be to blame. Could it be the ghostly Mr Carpenter, she wondered?

"It was an odd house really. It had just been renovated when we moved in there in August 1994, so it was spotless. However, all that autumn and winter, until we left the following January, the place was always full of flies. I spent a fortune on fly killer strips and aerosols but they just would not die. I was glad to leave really, but when the meters were read I had a real shock. I couldn't believe the electric bill for five months was so high. I used gas for cooking, heating and the hot water. It was just impossible to have used that much electricity running basically the lights, video, stereo and fridge. I appealed to the electricity company but they told me I would have to pay," said Sharon.

This has interesting parallels with the story of Georgina and Dean Rogers (see Chapter 11), who suffered huge bills when a ghost tapped into their power supply, and the case of Caroline Sutcliffe who lived in a small terraced house at Hunnyhill, Newport. The Vicar of Newport was called in to move on a ghost there, but when the quarter's electricity bill arrived, it was almost £800. (Read about it in Ghosts of the Isle of Wight III)

FOOTSTEPS IN THE NIGHT

Ghosts at an old three-storey house in Victoria Road, Cowes, can often be heard arguing, whispering and coughing. Their footsteps are heard late at night when they also rattle latches and handles, opening and closing doors.

Marie and Bob Tanner and their three sons became quite used to their ghosts' antics. "They are harmless, if a little irritating at times, but we can live with them," said Marie.

The family bought the Victorian house in 1987, and even before they had moved in Marie encountered one of the ghosts. "Bob and I were inspecting the property with an architect when I sat down in the front room for a rest. Suddenly I heard a voice whispering in my ear. It was a very loud whisper but I couldn't make out a single word. I wasn't frightened and it certainly didn't put me off the house," she said.

After they had moved into the house, Marie actually overheard a ghostly conversation. "I was upstairs in the bathroom, sitting on the loo when I heard voices. Again I couldn't understand a word they were saying but I could tell it was a woman and a man arguing. The voices seemed to be all around me and they were having a heated argument but the anger was controlled and repressed. The man was angry, the woman pleading. I was listening so hard trying to make out the words; it was painfully frustrating."

As the months went by, odd things started happening in the boys' bedrooms, where phantom hands would move drawers, opening and closing curtains while Marie was reading bedtime stories. One Saturday afternoon when Marie and Bob were alone in the house they heard the constant sound of a man's deep racking cough coming from upstairs.

"We would sometimes hear two distinct sets of footsteps, one with a light running tread, the other sounded much heavier as though someone was stomping about. We asked a medium round to tell us who or what was responsible for the haunting.

"He said there were two entities in the house, one a child, the other an older person. They seemed to be quite happy here and unless we wanted to get rid of them, they wished to stay in the house and would not do us any harm."

Despite this assurance, Marie had the fright of her life one November day in 1990, when she was in the kitchen cleaning dresses for a cocktail party. Her son Paul, then aged three, was in the house with her. "I heard

Paul running about upstairs in and out of my bedroom. I shouted to him to come downstairs. I could still hear him running about, so I shouted again 'Come downstairs right now'.

My Legs Turned to Jelly

"The footsteps came running down the stairs towards me.....but there was no-one there. The footsteps ran down the hall to the front door then back again to me. My legs just gave way, they turned to jelly but I somehow managed to get outside - and as I passed the lounge I saw Paul fast asleep on the settee!"

Sometimes the family would hear a loud thumping which sounded as though someone was stamping on the floor upstairs. Doors would open and bang shut. One day when Marie, who works as a nurse, was asleep in the empty house after a spell of night duty, she heard six distinct loud knocks on her door.

"The handle was being rattled impatiently. I was angry and rather frightened so I shouted at whatever it was to go away. It did," she said.

"I had the impression that many of the ghosts' pranks were deliberately being directed at me. One night I was in Paul's room because he wasn't feeling well. As I lay in bed there, I heard a woman's voice call 'Willie' three times, in a loud whisper. This was the first time I had heard the voice say anything clearly and it seemed to be coming from the corridor outside.

"At 1am I heard someone go into the bathroom and close the door, but when I went to investigate I found the light was off and the room empty." Marie stood out in the corridor willing and daring something else to happen but eventually her patience gave out and she went back to bed. "As I did so the footsteps started again, they stamped up and down right outside the door. It was quite deliberate and it was aimed at me. I think our ghosts have a sense of humour."

Although Marie and Bob have not seen their spectral guests, Paul, their youngest son certainly has. The first time he glimpsed a ghost he was sitting on the toilet and his worried parents rushed upstairs when they heard his screams. The terrified boy said he had seen a black shadowy figure walking across the bathroom towards him.

A few months later he saw the ghost again. This time it was standing on the landing outside the bathroom. The figure was that of a tall young man wearing a dark suit and white shirt. He stood with his legs crossed and his arms folded, appearing to be looking all around the hallway outside Paul's room, even up at the ceiling.

"He seemed nice but he didn't actually look at me. When I closed my eyes and looked away, the man vanished," said Paul.

Author's note: The ghosts are still active at the house. Paul seems to be the most psychic member of the family and is often aware of their presence. He was again woken by those heavy footsteps in May 2000.

Since I first spoke to the family in the mid 1990s, Marie and Bob have parted. Marie has learned that a curiously high number of other couples who once lived in the house have divorced or separated. Is it possible that the ghosts' unhappiness, the arguments and whispered pleadings the couple heard somehow poisoned the atmosphere, affecting their own relationship? Marie thinks perhaps that this was the case.

CHRISTMAS GHOST LIGHTS

A curious and inexplicable incident which took place in the early hours of Christmas morning more than fifty years ago, still haunts John Oakley. Although he was just a lad then, back in the late 1940s, he still puzzles over the events of that night.

"We were living in a cottage on the Debourne Manor estate at West Cowes, which we rented from the council. At about 2am on December 25, I heard my parents getting up. We kids were listening out for Father Christmas, so naturally we were curious to know what was going on."

His father, Jack Windsor Oakley, had seen the flickering light from a lantern outside the cottage, moving about a sunken grass ring in front of the manor house.

"Dad got dressed and went outside, thinking it must be old Miss Caws who had the farm nearby. Her cows sometimes got out and being an old-fashioned and eccentric lady, she would not have thought twice about going after them with an old lantern to light the way.

"My old man had not long got back from the war so he wasn't frightened of anything. He went out after this lantern and followed it right through the copse, out to the old stone wall in Baring Road. When the wavering light reached the wall, it went right through it and completely disappeared. When he got home again, Dad was quite puzzled by the whole thing. He was positive it was a lantern he had been following, although whoever - or whatever - was carrying it had made no noise at all. My mum had seen it too, so they knew they had not imagined it."

GHOST OF ILL TIDINGS

Whenever bad news was about to arrive, Joan Warner was always prepared for the worst. The night before any ill tidings arrived, she would receive a terrifying and unwelcome visitation from an unseen entity at her home in Haskell Road, Parkhurst.

The old block of flats formerly used by prison officers and their families has been torn down now, but in the early 1960s, Joan was used to spending nights alone there with the children, when her husband was working night duty. "It was odd because I never saw it, but it would pester me when I was going to hear bad news. I would be asleep and would awaken to feel this 'being' lying on top of me squeezing the breath out of me until I woke up. Then it would get off and I would hear it move out of the room and disappear."

This visitation would always presage bad news, such as a family fatality, a car crash, a close relative suffering a stroke, the dog getting run over. "I dreaded a visit from 'the thing' as I would worry myself sick until I knew what the next disaster was going to be," Joan said.

Happily, when the family moved out of the flat, she was never bothered again by the harbinger of bad news. Their new house at Park Road, Cowes, was haunted by a much more genial phantom, which was seen by Joan's young grandchildren. Emma was about eight at the time and she would sleep with Joan when she came to stay. One night she asked her grandmother, 'Why is that man staring at us from the corner of the room?'

The young girl told her disbelieving granny that the man was wearing a funny uniform and looked like a Roman soldier. "Frankly I thought she had dreamed the whole thing and laughed at her," confessed Joan. She completely forgot the strange episode and it was not until several years later when her youngest grandchild, Christopher, came to stay, that the apparition paid another visit. The youngster, then aged nine, told Joan he had seen a man in the corner of the room wearing a helmet, a leather top and a metal skirt!

Unknown to Joan, a lodger in the Park Road house also saw the apparition, which so unnerved him that he dived under the bedclothes and refused to come out until the first light of dawn. He complained that he had been disturbed by the ghostly soldier three nights in a row, and said it had leaned over his bed, looking directly into his face.

"When I left Park Road I walked into every bedroom and told the ghost our new address, adding that it was quite welcome to come with us. I did tell the people who bought the house that it had a ghost. I don't think they believed me. Perhaps they know better now," laughed Joan.

DEAD MAN WALKING

As the town of Cowes expanded during the nineteenth century, Northwood Cemetery, off Newport Road, was opened in 1855. Generations of townsfolk are interred there. But at least one does not rest easy in his grave.

It was a fine summer evening in 1993 as Shirley and Godfrey Butchers laid flowers on a family grave. The couple, who live at Debourne Manor Drive, Cowes, walked back along the main path through the cemetery to their car, past weathered headstones, memorials to the town's dead.

"It was still warm, the sun was coming through the trees and we were the only people there - or so we thought," said Shirley. "Suddenly in front of us we noticed a young man, aged in his mid to late twenties, coming towards us. We both said 'Good evening' to him as we passed.

A young man's ghost walks this path through Cowes Cemetery

He smiled in return, but did not speak.

"As he went by, we both turned and looked back at him. We couldn't see his legs. Where they should have been was just empty space. We stared at one another, quickly looked again, but the young man had vanished.

"It was so weird. He had looked real and solid enough for us to have wished him 'Good evening'. We were just a few feet apart when we passed, but it wasn't until Godfrey and I looked back that we became aware we could only see half his body.

"He was wearing a check shirt and what looked like the top of a pair of jeans. He was quite ordinary really and had been moving normally, as if walking. I don't know what instinct made us turn at the same time to look back at him, but I'm glad we both did. It was not frightening, just very strange. Godfrey has been visiting the cemetery since 1952 but this is the first time he has experienced anything like this."

THE FISHERMAN'S SPIRIT

It was August 1986 when Bryan Richardson, his wife Inge-Lise, and their seven year-old son Kenneth, moved into the two upper floors of a three-storey house built in the mid-1800s, close to the boatyards in Medina Road, Cowes.

"We lived there for 15 months. The first few months were fine, then one evening, when Kenneth was in bed and we were watching television in the front lounge, we both heard footsteps moving around in our bedroom directly above. I went upstairs as I thought Kenneth had woken. To my surprise he was fast asleep in the next room," said Bryan.

"The same thing happened a few weeks later, when we again heard the sound of footsteps which appeared to move around the room. These footsteps continued for some months; always in the evening. We didn't like them but we learned to live with them.

"One evening Kenneth was in bed and we were both watching television as usual, with the door open in case he woke. We suddenly looked at one another. I asked Inge-Lise, 'Have you just seen something?' She told me she had. I grabbed a pen and paper and said, 'Write it down'.

"I wrote down what I had seen, then we compared notes. We had both seen the figure of an elderly man in old clothes, which moved along the landing and up the stairs. Kenneth later told us he had also seen a similar image in his bedroom. Meanwhile, those footsteps continued.

"My wife and I were becoming more and more concerned. A few weeks later I was at home alone in the lounge at midday, when the footsteps started. This was followed by a tremendous pounding noise coming from upstairs. I am not normally a nervous man but I admit I broke into a cold sweat that day!

"I spoke to some of the workers at the boatyard, about the strange incidents, to see if they could throw any light on them. They just laughed and I didn't say any more.

"A few days later we were having a lie-in one Sunday morning when an image started to appear on the bedroom wall opposite the window. I woke my wife and as it became clearer, we realised it was an inverted, colour picture of the Duke of York pub across the road. It became so clear that we could see people walking in the picture, but it did not resemble the view we had from our bedroom window. This phenomenon lasted almost an hour before fading away. It appeared again a month later. This time we had visitors from East Sussex staying with us and I immediately dug them out of bed to come and witness it. They were as bewildered as we were by the strange picture."

Fred Peach and his wife Irene of Staplecross, who both saw the odd scene, which appeared to be a reverse image of the pub across the road, confirmed this.

Bryan continued, "The final straw came in the early hours of one morning. We both woke to the sound of footsteps walking around the bed. We didn't stir until they stopped. The next day we transferred into the back bedroom. Later we moved house. It was some time afterwards that we were having dinner with the owner of the house. He showed us some old photographs of the boatyard which had been taken at the turn of the century, before it was completely gutted by fire.

"The fire is believed to have been caused by a fisherman smoking his pipe while mending his nets. The long-dead fisherman lived in that house.... And I believe he still does."

Author's note: The boatyard and house in Medina Road have since been sold. When asked about the ghost, owner Lawrence Boarer said, "We call him 'Old Marley'. He's supposed to have been around for years. I have never seen or heard him though, and the tenants in the house now have had no problems with him. All is quiet there now."

The Four Seasons watch over Union Street at Ryde

Chapter Six

HAUNTED RYDE

SPIRITS AT YELF'S

The sounds of pots and pans being hurled around the kitchen of Yelf's Hotel, Ryde, are common. Staff there are used to loud bangs and crashes late at night, but they know it's not the chef having a tantrum. It's the hotel ghost letting off steam.

The old hotel and coaching inn half-way down Union Street was originally built by Robert Yelf in 1801, when the road was little more than a track joining upper and lower Ryde. As the town grew, thanks to the new pier, Yelf's quickly became one of the best-known family and commercial hotels in Ryde.

That commotion in the kitchen has been happening for many years, and general manager of the hotel, Lin Simmonds, heard it countless times. "It sounds like metal pots and pans being thrown around, but when you go in, there's never anything out of place. We are all used to it - but we don't lock up at night or go in to make early 6.30am breakfast alone. We always go in twos.... just in case."

Former duty manager, Sue Hunt, who has since left, agreed, "We don't lock up alone because of 'The Ghost', it's just an accepted thing."

Although whatever haunts the hotel is rarely seen, staff agree the presence is masculine, and that it seems strongest in the basement storeroom area by the kitchen stairs. It was on these stairs that a kitchen porter felt a ghostly touch on her arm; while in the nearby walk-in fridge, a duty manager found herself locked in.

"It was very strange because these doors have a handle on the inside so that this cannot happen. But the door just wouldn't open, and her screams for help weren't heard until the chef noticed she had been missing for some time," said Sue.

Guests at the hotel are unaware of the ghostly activity, which seems confined to the kitchens and service area. "You often feel you are being watched and catch a glimpse of something moving in that basement, but you never see it clearly," added Sue.

Spirits are served here at the haunted Yelf's Hotel, Ryde

PHANTOM FOR ALL SEASONS

A few doors down Union Street from Yelf's, look upwards at the statues on top of five storey Regina House. Just below the Royal Victoria Arcade, this architectural fantasy commonly known as the Four Seasons, has watched over the town's fortunes for more than 130 years.

Minor royalty were frequent visitors there to sit for photographic portraits, for Cornelius Jabez Hughes who built Regina House in 1865, was photographer to Her Majesty Queen Victoria at Osborne House. Hughes went into partnership with Gustav Mullins - their names can still be seen on a large enamel sign on the side of the building - and they were in great demand with the nobility as top society photographers.

In those days, the ground floor, now occupied by Bernard Mitchell, Jewellers, and Renegade, a shop specialising in American Western memorabilia, was used for reception rooms and studios. The first floor, with 12ft high ceilings to dispel noxious photographic chemical fumes, housed more studios and dark rooms. Hot water pipes centrally heated all 25 rooms, while the crowning glory of Regina House was the set of statues depicting the Four Seasons.

None of this however explains why first and second floor rooms overlooking the street should be haunted by the warm, aromatic smell of perfume and old-fashioned tobacco. Shortly after Nigel Foskett moved into his first floor flat in 1995, he noticed the pungent aroma of tobacco in the bedroom.

"There was nothing creepy about it at all. I liked the smell. It always came late at night, usually around 11.30pm. Whatever caused it came in cycles. It could be there every night for a couple of weeks, then wouldn't come again for a month or so. It was so strong that it was just as if a tobacco tin had been opened under your nose," said Nigel. "If I had to be haunted by a smell, I suppose I'm lucky it wasn't the odour of those old chemical fumes!"

In March 2000, Nigel, his wife and their baby daughter, moved to a flat on the top floor where, so far, they have been free from phantom smells. However, the elderly lady who has lived in the second floor flat for the past 40 years, told Nigel she had noticed the strong smells of tobacco smoke and perfume so often that she was quite used to them. The aromas only ever manifested in one particular room - at the front of the building directly above the room where Nigel also experienced the same phenomenon.

THE SPECTRAL SOLDIER

The following story involving a Ryde church was investigated by members of the Society for Psychical Research a century ago......

Approaching the town from the sea, one of the first buildings to catch the eye is All Saints Parish Church in Queens Road, an imposing example of Victorian architecture consecrated in 1872. Its architect, George Gilbert Scott, also designed the Royal Albert Hall, the Albert Memorial and St Pancras Station.

During Easter 1900 Amelia Raynham, a prominent operatic soprano, was staying with friends at Appley Park. Normally her visits to the Island were a source of great pleasure, but this time she was grieving for her brother George, a cavalry officer reported missing in the battle of Spion Kop, one of the bloodiest engagements of the Boer War.

With her friend Marjorie Banks of Newport, she visited the church and, sitting in a pew near the altar, the women discussed what might have happened to George. As they were quite alone in the church, both women turned to see who had come in when the door creaked open.

*A ghostly soldier was seen here at
All Saints Parish Church, Ryde*

They heard it close again but to their surprise, no one appeared, although they clearly heard footsteps walk past them down the nave, right up to the altar. There the footsteps, made by boots with spurs, stopped.

Puzzled, the women went to investigate, but the church was completely empty. Just as they were about to leave, those strange, invisible boot-steps sounded again. Near the altar stood an officer with head bowed, facing the window. The soldier turned and Amelia Raynham realised it was her missing brother.

With echoing footsteps he walked down the aisle towards her, his arms outstretched. She ran to meet him, but as she came close she stopped suddenly. For his face was covered in blood from a terrible head wound; his gore-soaked jacket was stained with mud. As she gazed in horror, the figure vanished.

Marjorie Banks had been watching all this time and she ran to where her friend stood sobbing. She searched all the nearby pews, but could find no trace of the soldier, who for a few moments had appeared real and solid to both women.

The sighting was reported to and later discussed by members of the Society for Psychical Research. They concluded that Amelia Raynham may have been able to see her dead brother materialise in the church because she had been thinking about him in surroundings which held happy memories for both of them. And, unusually, the materialisation had been so powerful that it had also been visible to Marjorie Banks, a telepathically unconnected witness.

SCHOOL FOR SPIRITS

Whenever Jill Atkinson tried to call the register at her playschool in Ryde, the numbers never seemed to tally. It should not have been difficult for four members of staff to check there were 60 children present.... but sometimes it was downright impossible.

"With four of us counting it could take up to 20 minutes. There always seemed to be too many children present," said a very puzzled Jill.

Then other curious things started happening at the little school. In October 1993 Jill glimpsed a little fair-haired child, about five years old, wearing a white shirt, black trousers and waistcoat, hurrying round a corner out of the classroom. "I went after him to see where he was going. I thought he was one of mine, but he simply disappeared in the foyer between two rooms."

The atmosphere at the school seemed to become more and more "charged". Jill is psychically receptive and when a new assistant with similar sensitivity joined the staff, matters quickly came to a head.

"We were sitting with a group of children at a table when a black shape loomed out of the wall and moved in front of me. I felt that it was a female presence. The room went very, very cold, the whole atmosphere changed and it became unpleasant and creepy," she shuddered. Thankfully none of the children noticed the shadow, but Jill's new assistant had seen it and had also felt that sudden penetrating coldness.

"After that things became more difficult and I always had the impression that there were other spirits there. In the end I found the name of a medium in the County Press and asked her to come to give us some advice. By this time I was feeling reluctant to even enter the school. The medium came one afternoon when the children were not around.

"She told us that there were two resident spirits, Annabel and Josef, little ghost children who had been attracted by the presence of other living children of a similar age.

"The medium said that Annabel had been killed in an air raid on her school in Leipzig during the last war. Her little friend, Josef, had survived, but had died in a later raid."

A bewildered Jill asked why on earth the children had attached themselves to her school more than 50 years after they had died.

The medium explained that the little earthbound spirits were simply attracted to the living children and were very happy playing among them.

"I don't know if 'my' children could actually see the little ghosts. I do believe some of them could but didn't realise there was anything odd about it. I'm sure one little boy was a 'seer'. He would often look past me and smile at something I couldn't see."

The medium explained to Jill that the little spirits were earthbound. She would try to send them on to where they should go, she said.

"They told her they would go but asked if they could come back to visit if they promised to be good. In the middle of all this I burst into tears for no apparent reason. The medium explained gently that the little spirits had just kissed me goodbye.

"I felt really sad that I had sent them away. The medium assured me that they were now where they should be and that other loving spirits had come to show them the way. However, they do come back to visit us occasionally. I always know when Annabel and Josef are around. I feel jumpy and the children are more noisy and mischievous. I also find pools of water all over the place as the little spirits seem to be extremely fond of playing with water."

Annabel and Josef were not the only entities the medium found at the school. She also made contact with Hazel, an ancient white witch who lived in the third century. Hazel, she claimed, was a spirit guide and guardian of the children, and would certainly not submit to being "sent on" as Annabel and Josef had been. It was Hazel's shade that Jill and her assistant had glimpsed that day in the classroom.

Hazel is particularly active whenever a new child joins the school, especially if they are upset or tearful. She is always on hand to comfort them. "I now feel that I can call on her at any time to lend a hand," smiled Jill.

Since the medium's visit Jill has felt much happier about the school and its uninvited visitors; she always remembers to greet Hazel when she arrives each morning.

Jill and other members of staff often notice pungent smells around the school. Strong pipe smoke, apple blossom and other floral fragrances waft around the corridors. So too does another distinctive odour - a strong smell of urine. "I wonder if it is another child. It seems to cling very close to you and follows you around all day," Jill said.

Sometimes staff hear the sound of muffled conversations coming from the foyer area, but they can never make out any words in the ghostly conversations. They occasionally have to speak sharply to the spirits telling them to return small items that they have purloined.

"We put a pen or ruler down and it simply vanishes. It really is quite infuriating. I have to speak very quietly, in case the children think I've gone mad, but I firmly tell whoever has done it return the things at once."

As the new term started in September 1994, the unseen visitors were still about. Some children talked about the 'Green Girl' and looked bewildered when she disappeared. The medium had told Jill that Annabel wore a green skirt, so perhaps it was her spirit they could see.

"We also have regular visits from other ghosts. The most recent is a lady wearing a beige raincoat. These spirits seem to be very interested in our PE lessons. I wish they would help dress the children. It would certainly make life much easier!"

Jill concluded, "There is obviously something about the school building which attracts spirits but they don't bother the staff or children. There is certainly nothing sinister here, just idle curiosity and playfulness, with Hazel, our spirit guide to watch over things!"

HAUNTING AT HAYLANDS

Even at their home near Haylands, which was built on the site of an old pair of cottages, Jill and her family could not escape the supernatural.

Her son clearly saw a little ghost wearing a blue shirt and short trousers, which rushed across the landing upstairs one night. On another occasion in the early hours of the morning, he heard the sound of voices coming from the lounge below and went to investigate. Three times he went downstairs and three times he opened the door to find the room silent and empty.

Another night, something completely reorganised the family's lounge, moving furniture and stacking daughter Lucy's birthday cards into a pyramid. Lucy complained of unseen hands stroking her hair in the night and of a light-fingered entity which seemed to delight in taking her personal belongings - always something coloured black. These items including combs, a scarf and leggings completely disappeared, never to be seen again.

This house has now been sold and the family has moved into a flat above Jill's new expanded nursery school premises in a large Victorian villa at Ryde. The former playschool building has reverted to its previous use as a dancing school.

Did any of the spirits move with you? I inquired. "They didn't need to," Jill admitted, "The house had already got a few of its own. When we moved in there was a very sad atmosphere. The rooms felt very cold; we couldn't heat them up at all.

"I finally got in touch with Wendy, the medium I had used at the playschool. She made contact with the earthbound spirit of a servant who had lived and worked here for two Victorian doctors, and with the spirit of a soldier who was killed in World War Two. They have moved on now and the place feels warmer and happy again."

A PHANTOM WARDROBE?

When Dawn Hicks moved into the basement flat of a large Victorian villa in John Street, Ryde, she took an instant dislike to the dark, old-fashioned furniture which went with the apartment, quickly replacing it with modern pieces of her own choosing. So when she awoke in the early hours of the morning some two months later, Dawn was startled to find that the old furniture had come back.

Not only was the bedroom full of ugly antiquated furnishings again, there, standing near the bed, was the ghost of an elderly man, beckoning Dawn to follow him.

"I was absolutely petrified. At first I just didn't know where I was. Then I recognised an old table, sideboard and chairs I had got rid of when I moved into the flat. The room wasn't furnished as a bedroom any more; it looked more like a parlour or some sort of dining room.

"The old gentleman, who appeared to be in his sixties, seemed to be aware of me. He looked at me with a faint smile and with his hand outstretched, beckoned me with a finger. He was wearing strange old-fashioned clothes and his jacket was dark green. The figure was quite solid and real; I couldn't see through him. I had the strangest feeling that I had somehow gone back in time, although I was still in my bed."

Dawn tried to wake her fiance who was sleeping peacefully beside her. "I shook him and told him there was somebody in the room and that it was a ghost. He just told me I was dreaming and went back to sleep."

At this point Dawn was so overcome with terror that she pulled the bedclothes over her head and didn't emerge until the first light of the early summer sun touched the room.

"Everything was back to normal again the next morning. I moved out of the flat soon afterwards, but I sometimes wonder what would have happened if I had got out of bed that night and followed the ghost. If I had gone with him would I have ever found my way back .....?"

THE WAR-TIME GHOST

A dowdy looking ghost wearing 1940s-style clothing appeared for a couple of minutes one night in January 1999, then vanished again as silently as she had come.

It was a clear, cold night, as Wendy Mitchell walked along Cross Street to her home in nearby George Street, Ryde. "It was about 10.10pm and the town was very quiet. There was no traffic around and as I don't like being out on my own at night, I was pleased to see someone walking ahead of me.

"It was a woman dressed in what looked like a 1940s-style suit with a hairstyle to match. She was quite short, just over five feet tall, solid and stocky looking. The street lights are bright there and I could clearly make out her dowdy clothes and darkish grey-brown hair. A lady of late

middle age, she wasn't moving very fast but I couldn't hear the sound of her footsteps, although we were only a few yards apart.

"Just past the Union Lane turning she disappeared. Suddenly. She didn't fade; she was there one second, gone the next. It was quite extraordinary! I was too amazed to be frightened. I tried to persuade myself that I must have imagined her... but I know I didn't," Wendy said.

A dowdy ghost appeared in Cross Street, Ryde

THE HAUNTED BED & BREAKFAST

This next story happened some years ago in Ryde. Unfortunately the family concerned cannot remember the address of the guest house, which was chosen from that year's Holiday Guide. It was towards the outskirts of town and there were two rows of terraced houses. Their accommodation was in a cottage in the middle of the right-hand side of the road, with a playing field behind. Perhaps *you* can identify it.....

It was the Gibbon family's first visit to the Isle of Wight, and their B&B accommodation was not quite what they had hoped for. They were realistic enough not to expect luxury or even sea views for what they were paying. But they never dreamed they would have to share their rooms in the little terraced guest house with a ghost.

"By the end of the week we were all sleeping together in one room. We were terrified and if we could have possibly afforded to find somewhere else to stay, we would have left immediately," recalled Allan Gibbon.

With his wife Sylvia and their two children, Dene, seven, and Trudy, five, the family had driven from Manchester for a week at the seaside, in August 1967.

"We didn't have much money and this holiday, our first with the children, had been paid for by my in-laws," admitted Allan. "The elderly landlady lived there on her own and we were her only guests."

After their long journey the children went early to bed, but Trudy was soon in her parents' room, crying wildly that arms were coming out of the wall trying to grab her. Dismissing this as the result of over-excitement and an unfamiliar room, Allan and Sylvia tucked her up in bed with them for the rest of the night.

However the next night Dene came running in, sobbing, with a similar story. He told his parents that two solid arms had come out of the wall and were trying to reach his bed. "We didn't like to say anything to our landlady in case she thought we were mad, and anyway, I had always been extremely sceptical about ghosts and the like," Allan said.

His doubt in the supernatural was put to the test the next night when he woke to find a hooded figure at the foot of the bed. It was a young woman about 19 or 20 years of age and she stood motionless, staring straight at him.

She was clearly visible in the light from a street lamp outside and the figure also seemed to glow with its own soft radiance. Less than six feet

away, the strange visitor was almost leaning on the end of the bed. "Her face was expressionless, but she had a beautiful, flawless complexion, and she wore a deep blue velvet cloak. She seemed aware of me and I thought she was about to speak. She started to glide across the bottom of the bed towards a heavy old wardrobe which she disappeared into."

Suddenly all those children's stories of ghostly arms didn't seem so far-fetched. "I was petrified. I went so rigid that my wife woke and asked what the matter was. My hair was literally standing on end."

Ryde pictured in the mid 1960s, when the Gibbon family stayed at a haunted bed and breakfast

Still the family said nothing to their landlady! They did however discover that she was a keen Spiritualist, and Allan and Sylvia wondered if this could account for the stray spirits in their lodgings.

"If we could have afforded to go somewhere else we would have been out of there like a shot. Unfortunately we had paid for the week and I don't think we would have got our money back if we had complained that we were sharing with a ghost.

"We spent the remaining nights huddled together in one bed with the children, and were relieved when the holiday was over. It was an experience none of us can forget. It was so vivid and real."

Allan and Sylvia now run their own guest house, the Ferndene, at Keswick in the Lake District. As they ask visitors if they have enjoyed their stay, they sometimes smile wryly at their own haunted holiday memories and wonder how many other guests at that Ryde bed and breakfast experienced such ghostly hospitality?

Old St Helens Church tower pictured in the year 1900

Chapter Seven

ROADS TO NOWHERE

A STEP BACK IN TIME?

It was a little after 10am on Tuesday, 16 June 1999, when Noeline and Michael Sleat got off the bus at the top of Springvale Road. The couple from Shirley near Croydon, were holidaying on the Island and today they were on their way to visit the Flamingo Park tourist attraction at Seaview.

It was a beautiful sunny day and the countryside was at its best. As they strolled down the lane, Noeline and Michael paused to admire a large house surrounded by lawns, where a group of children were playing with what looked like a football. The youngsters, who were aged about eight or nine, were in a circle. Nearby were some old-fashioned hockey sticks and schoolbags.

"One of the little lads was wearing antiquated breeches and a girl beside him was in an old-fashioned brown gymslip. Another child, a rather tubby little boy, caught my eye as he wore a bright yellow shirt," said Noeline. "We could hear noise coming from the children but we could not make out any words. Curiously, although the ball was being kicked it did not appear to go anywhere. It was like watching a video constantly replaying. I have never experienced anything quite like it.

"As we walked on down the lane, we saw two men with a very old-fashioned car, but they didn't look at us or acknowledge us when we called out 'Good Morning'. We were soon at the Flamingo Park, which was already busy, although we hadn't seen any traffic on the way there. However, we soon forgot our odd experience and spent an enjoyable couple of hours there, leaving just after midday to walk back to the bus stop.

"When we reached that lovely old house we were surprised to see the noisy group of children was still there. They hadn't moved at all. I said to my husband, 'Look. How odd!' but as he turned his head to see, they suddenly disappeared.

"It was like switching a television off. One moment they were sitting there, then they were gone. We were so startled by the experience that we legged it quickly up the lane to wait for the next bus. Fortunately we didn't have to wait long. We just wanted to get away from there. I don't know what we witnessed - whether it was a moment from the past or whether we actually slipped momentarily back in time. Whatever it was, I don't ever want to do it again!"

DARK FIGURE AT THE DUVER

A mysterious dark figure was seen gliding along the sea wall at St Helens, one clear moonlit night. But as it reached the remains of the old church tower there, it disappeared, leaving the three young men who had been observing its progress mystified.

Richard Cattell clearly recalls that early January night in 1995 when he and his friends were sitting in their car at the Duver listening to the car stereo.

"It was about 8pm and we were parked on the sea wall near the café. The place was deserted; there was no-one else around. Suddenly we noticed a strange, dark figure gliding along the wall, close to the car. It was just a shape, like the outline of a body. We couldn't see any features like hands or feet, but all of us saw it. As we watched, it glided towards the old church tower, then vanished."

Puzzled by what they had just seen, Richard and the others got out of the car and walked towards the old tower to try to find out where the figure had disappeared to. But the place was shuttered and deserted. They were alone by the ruined church. Suddenly the Duver did not seem a good place to be on a still, clear January night.

The buttressed thirteenth century tower is all that remains of the old Duver Church at St Helens; the remainder was swept into the sea. As early as the sixteenth century, the church was reported to be in a shameful state but little was done to halt its decline. It finally collapsed in November 1703 leaving just the tower, which has since become a seamark.

OLD CHURCH ST HELENS

The ill-fated church and its tower have long been a place of legend. One of its priests, the fourteenth century monk Aymo, brought shame on the church and the nearby Priory by worshipping the devil. Satanic rites were performed on the altar of the church and he is said to have led a coven of black witches who met there.

Aymo defied excommunication, continuing to preach in his deserted church, although the congregation had long since fled, believing the place to be cursed. This may explain why the church was allowed to fall into such disrepair that it was washed into the sea.

In 1784 workmen from Portsmouth arrived to strengthen what was left of the tower and to paint the seaward side white. The foreman was astonished to find a little old-fashioned gentleman in tight leather shorts and woollen stockings asleep on top of the tower. As he called his men to come and look, the old man, angered at being disturbed, cursed the workmen. They would suffer the same fate as an earlier party of masons who had originally built the tower, he predicted.

The workmen thought it a big joke, but when the time came for them to return to the mainland they remembered his words and grew nervous. Rightly so, for after they set sail for Portsmouth in their boat, they were never seen again.

HAUNTING MELODY

A haunting melody being sung by a ghost woke Ian Bartlett early on Christmas morning in 1992. It was the voice of a young woman singing unaccompanied and the sound seemed to be coming from an arched window high up on the bedroom wall.

Ian and his girlfriend Louisa, who have since married, were living at the time in Ducie Avenue, Bembridge, in a house which was built by Bruce Ismay, owner of the White Star Line, whose great liner the Titanic sank on her maiden voyage. The house was one of five in the road, which Mr Ismay had ordered to be built for his five daughters.

It was precisely 3.20am on December 25, when Ian first heard the ghostly strains of what sounded like 'Greensleeves' floating around the room. "It was a gorgeous voice and sounded as if the singer was a woman of between 30 and 40 who was standing at the window. It lasted for about 15 seconds and disappeared as suddenly as it had begun."

As well as a ghostly cat, which could often be heard jumping from her favourite window ledge upstairs, the figure of a little old lady terrified Louisa's sister one night by sitting cross-legged on the end of her bed.

"My sister was woken in the early hours by the weight of someone on the end of the bed. She opened her eyes to see a little elderly woman, sitting cross-legged just a few feet away. The figure apparently spoke, for my sister heard a voice say, 'Do not worry dear, I am not going to hurt you'."

Not at all reassured by this, Louisa's sister did what most people would have done. She hid under the bedclothes until she was certain the ghost had gone!

PHANTOMS ON THE ROAD

Reports of ghosts appearing on Isle of Wight roads frequently come my way. So remember, keep your eyes open. That figure at the side of the road may not be what it seems. Here are just a few of the sightings:

A Misty Figure

Victor and Linda Hipkiss of South Wales were holidaying on the Island in July 1999, when they encountered the misty figure of a monk in Main Road, Arreton, just before noon. The road was quiet and Linda noticed an elderly man in a dark robe, with a white cord round the waist, standing at the side of the road. The man, whom she took to be a monk looked old and unwell so she turned to her husband to suggest they should stop to ask if he needed help. "What monk"? he asked.

No one apart from Linda had seen him, and as she looked back to point him out, the road was empty. The figure had vanished.

Staddlestones Spectre

Carol Prince was driving through Ashey on her way home from work in Ryde, at 10.15pm one night, when she saw an old lady in the road trying to flag her down. Carol's 15-year-old daughter, Cindy, called out to her mother to stop.

"I could see her quite clearly in the headlights. She was tall, with lank grey hair and glasses and she wore a check jacket. But some sixth sense told me not to stop and to keep driving. There was something not right about her."

Carol's instinct was later proved right. She later discovered that a number of other motorists had often seen the same figure at that spot near Staddlestones Garage trying to flag them down. A Ryde police officer later confirmed that a number of calls about her had been logged. "Some people do ring us when they have seen her, but we think it's a ghost," Carol was told.

Phantom Jogger

Nick Barnes of Portsmouth had a terrifying experience when the front of his car went through a jogger one evening as he and a friend were driving from Rookley towards Ventnor. Nick was a confirmed sceptic who laughed at the idea of ghosts until he encountered this one.

"I saw him 200-300 yards in front of me. He was dressed in a blue jogging top and trainers and was running along the road. I slowed down but he suddenly crossed over in front of the car and I went through him. The car suddenly became freezing cold; so icy cold that I had tears in my eyes. It was a very eerie feeling. There was no sign of the figure. I checked everywhere but he had vanished."

Both Nick and his friend had clearly seen the solid-seeming jogger. Both were both baffled and very shaken by their experience.

Ghost of Gallows Hill

June Walker of Ventnor had to swerve sharply to avoid hitting a man walking down Gallows Hill, near Arreton on 20 August 1997. It was 5.45am and she was driving home after taking her husband to catch the ferry at East Cowes.

The aptly-named Gallows Hill at Arreton, where ghosts are seen

"I had to swerve to miss hitting the man who was walking by the chalk pit, but when I looked in my rear view mirror and wing mirrors, there was no-one there. I slowed right down but he had vanished. He had been dressed in old-style clothing; a leather waistcoat and dark breeches with heavy boots.

"I never saw his face because when I came alongside him and glanced sideways he was gone. He seemed to be carrying something like a sack or bag over his left shoulder. I was quite perturbed by my experience, but when I told my husband he laughed and said I must have been half-asleep. But I know I wasn't!" protested June.

In fact, sightings of a ghostly figure at Gallows Hill have been reported for years. It is thought to be that of Michal Morey, the murderous woodcutter, who hacked his young grandson to death in 1736, and who was executed for his crime at Winchester. His body was brought back to Arreton to be hung in a corpse cage on the public gibbet outside the Hare and Hounds pub. Other people have described seeing his figure trudging along the road.....carrying an axe wrapped in cloth over his shoulder. (Read the accounts in the Original Ghosts of the IW)

The Cowleaze Ghost

It was a clear moonlit November night when Louisa Pratt and two friends collided with the ghost of a Victorian farmer on a lonely road just outside Shanklin.

"We were on our way to Ventnor for a drink at the Spyglass Inn at about 9pm. There was hardly any traffic on the roads. Ian Bartlett was driving and I was sitting in the back with my feet up on the seat. As we went up Cowleaze Hill there was a tremendous wallop on the side of the car as though we had been hit by something," said Louisa, who has since become Mrs Bartlett.

In the headlights she could see the figure of a man with his arm raised. He was nicely dressed, but in a strange old-fashioned way more appropriate to Victorian times than the 1990s, with short breeches, leather leggings, jacket and waistcoat.

"I seem to remember a small white dog in the road and I looked at Ian and said, 'Oh my God, we have hit the dog'. At this, Ian and front-seat passenger Tim Grafton turned round and asked what on earth I was talking about.

"Look at that man, he is waving his stick at us. I think we have run over his dog," Louisa told the puzzled pair. "They could not see a thing.

To them the road was completely empty and they could not understand why I was so upset."

Strangely however, the two men had heard the loud bang on the side of the car, but although they turned back and stopped to see if they had hit anything, there was no sign of that ghostly farmer and his little terrier.

A Bloody Apparition

The bloody apparition of a man which appeared in front of him in the road at Chale, so terrified Steven Anker that he still sees it in his dreams. The ghost, which materialised at about 10.30pm one summer evening in 1990, was wearing dark trousers and a light coloured shirt, which was heavily bloodstained.

Steven, then aged 17, and his two friends, Steven Phillips and Steven Avey, had been walking home up Blythe Shute after a game of pool at the nearby pub. There was little traffic about that night, and Steven Anker, who had been lagging a few yards behind the others, was dawdling along and looking down at the road when he caught sight of something just in front of him. "I thought at first it was one of my friends I was just about to walk into. Then I noticed the bloodstains.....

"The figure which had its back towards me appeared quite solid. It was definitely a man who was not very tall and he looked as if he was trying to pull himself up off the ground. He lurched across the road, sort of dragging his leg and I thought he was going to fall over. As I stood there watching, he just faded away," said Steven, who by this time was in a state of shock.

"My heart was really thumping; I was petrified. I couldn't speak. I just took off and ran for my life as fast as my legs would carry me, back down the hill, until I reached the village pub, the Wight Mouse, again."

The other two Stevens who had not seen the ghost at all couldn't understand what had come over their friend. They followed him down the hill and because he appeared to be in such a bad state, they rang his mother, Gwen Anker, to come and fetch him.

Gwen recalls that her son was as white as a sheet and shaking when she arrived. "He was in shock and I was quite worried about him," she admitted. "We could hardly believe what had happened. However we started to look for a possible reason for what Steven had experienced. We discovered that many years ago there had been a hit and run accident on that same stretch of road.

"A local man walking along Blythe Shute had apparently been struck by a car which failed to stop. Although in a bad way, he had managed to drag himself across the road to his home nearby, where he died from his injuries," Gwen said.

Did this man's mortally wounded apparition appear to young Steven for a brief instant on that dark summer's night? He certainly believes it did and vivid nightmares are a reminder of his awful experience.

A Collision seemed Inevitable

For one heart-stopping moment, Joan Cotton thought her husband was going to hit the little Morris 1100 car which loomed out of the darkness in front of them.

It was about 9pm on a winter's night in 1990 and the couple were driving across the Downs road towards Newport. As they neared the junction with Knighton Shute, which winds down towards the long-vanished and much-haunted manor of Knighton Gorges, Joan saw a dark coloured, old-fashioned Morris which had stopped in the road in front of them. Realising a collision was inevitable, Joan grabbed her bag and clung for dear life to her seat, waiting for the crash.

It never came. Instead they drove right through the little car and as Joan let out an exclamation of relief, her husband asked what on earth was wrong.

Incredibly, he had not seen a thing. He had absolutely no idea that they had just driven through what Joan now knows was a ghost-car. She looked back immediately, but the road behind them was completely empty.

However, she knows that something very strange happened that night, and can clearly remember seeing the driver standing in the road by the open car door. "He was a young lad, who hardly looked old enough to be driving. He was blonde with a pert, pretty little nose. He was wearing a hand-knitted grey-blue jumper, and I could even see the ribbing as we drove right through the car," recalled Joan.

"What he was doing there I have no idea. But I do wonder whether a young man was ever killed at that spot, in an accident involving a Morris 1100."

Chapter Eight

SHADES OF OLD NEWPORT

BIZARRE EVENTS AT THE BUGLE

For centuries it was the principal coaching inn and hotel in the Island's market town and main departure point for stagecoaches. Described as the 'best and chief hostelrie in Newport', the Bugle Inn stood at the northern end of St James' Square until its abrupt closure in 1989. Five hundred years of history vanished overnight as dining rooms and bars, bedrooms and stable yard were converted into shops, offices and a car park.

Thought to date back to 1480 and originally known as The Bull, the ancient inn was used as the headquarters of the Parliamentary Commissioners in 1648 at the time of negotiations with King Charles I over the Treaty of Newport.

Local legend has it that in June 1621, an Island nobleman was mortally wounded in a sword fight in the street outside and carried to the stables behind The Bugle, where he died from his wounds. His ghost is said to be connected with poltergeist activity in the former hotel kitchens, which were built over part of those stables. As recently as the 1960s, pots and pans were thrown across the room by unseen hands, while staff saw the tall figure of a man standing, motionless, by the kitchen wall.

Following the Bugle's sudden closure, the ground floor was converted into shops with Mothercare and Ottakar's Bookshop opening there. The upper floors, now known as Bugle House, became offices which are now occupied by various departments of the Isle of Wight Council.

Many alterations were made to the building; the interior is now a busy, modern workplace. It's certainly not the sort of place you would expect to find a ghost - but a catalogue of bizarre events which occurred there in the late 1990s, completely baffled staff, managers, computer specialists, telecom troubleshooters and even the local police.

Only two psychics who were called in as a last resort to investigate, were undaunted by the strange goings-on at Bugle House. The manager there takes up the story:

Bizarre events at the old Bugle Hotel perplexed staff here in the 21st Century

"I'm not a believer in ghosts and I'm very sceptical myself. Initially I suspected a practical joker or even a malicious hoaxer - but now I'm keeping a very open mind...

"It started in autumn 1998. Paperwork and documents would vanish and turn up later somewhere else. Piles of envelopes went missing; an empty box moved around the offices at night. Small objects flew across the room, hurled with such force that they bounced off walls; small coins, usually 20p, 10p, 2p and 1p pieces started to appear through ceilings and walls. Two of the staff suffered particularly from this. We amassed about £5 in small change this way," she said.

"A computer engineer who was hit by a flying missile, refused to work here again. Female cleaners left because they had such bad experiences, being particularly frightened in the area around the first-floor toilets and kitchen.

"Doors locked themselves from the inside trapping people on several occasions. Finally the cleaners refused to work here and the company sent two men instead.

"My workforce had the jitters. Some staff would not go to the kitchen or toilet on their own - they went everywhere in pairs. We would come into work in the morning to find leads had been pulled out of the back of the computers and on one occasion, the computer was sitting on a chair in the centre of the room, with every wire disconnected. At first we suspected intruders, but the room was locked, windows secure, and protected by a surveillance camera. Police investigated but were unable to throw any light on the mystery. Actually they thought it was a hoot once they heard that a ghost might be the suspect," she said.

BT engineers were baffled

"Then something started to interfere with the telephone system to such an extent that BT were completely baffled. After months of investigations and daily visits, as well as two complete new telephone control systems with new phones, they could not solve it. BT were never able to give us a satisfactory answer and no cause was ever found, although we got to know the engineers very well.

"At one stage, we thought we had a serious problem with a computer hacker when our phones started calling themselves. When we looked at the bill there were pages and pages of calls - to our own number - it was crazy. One day there were over 800 calls to the speaking clock.

The calls would jump around the office, often seeming to focus on phones used by the two members of staff who had also been on the receiving end of the coins. In desperation BT told us to disconnect the fridge in case it was interfering with the system. Then they suggested that one of the girls should sit on an electrostatic shield in case she was somehow causing the problem!

"One day a call was actually made from my telephone when I was sitting in my office with a BT engineer. At the height of the activity it took eight of us to keep the phone lines clear, answering call after call. All our lines were blocked with calls, often from the same numbers. The main control centre of the British Transport Police was one of the regular callers; we had hundreds from them.

"Then we started getting calls from countries all over the world. If it hadn't been so exasperating it was almost a running joke; we had a map of the world on the wall and actually put stickers on each country we had received calls from.

"It was mayhem from 8.30am until about 11am, then it would subside, only to start again after lunch. This went on for months.

Sometimes there was a gap of a month or two, then it would start up again. There was incredible tension in the office. People all over the council knew of our problems and would joke, 'How's the ghost today?'

"Something had to be done. Finally, in early 1999 we called in a local medium, Ivy Griffiths. She arrived with fellow psychic, Wilma Tait. They sat in my office and listened to the story, then they 'tuned in' to a presence in the building, which they felt was that of a very young woman or child. They suggested we should leave something in the corner for her to play with, to distract her, or keep her occupied.

"They also talked to staff whom they felt were unwittingly attracting the attention of this mischievous, restless spirit. Ivy and Wilma said they would try to move her on 'towards the light' and since then we have had no major occurrences. It could just be coincidence. I really don't know."

Just before Christmas 1999, the manager and her staff noticed soap was disappearing at an alarming rate from that first-floor toilet. "We were getting through several bars or pump dispensers a week. Soap was vanishing within an hour of being put there, and dispensers were completely emptied overnight.

"We joked that at least we had a very clean ghost. Finally one of my staff had a few words with the ghost, asking it politely to leave the soap alone. It did, for the soap 'drain' has now ceased and calm has returned … for now."

THE FACELESS FIGURE

This rambling property in Lugley Street has a long and interesting history. Built around 1604, it was originally a town house for Mr Grey, a local gentleman. When King Charles I stayed in the old Newport Grammar School, almost directly opposite, for several months in 1648 while the Treaty of Newport was negotiated, it is recorded that he visited the residence of Mr Grey.

Braunstone House, with its courtyard garden and outbuildings, was remodelled in Regency times and traces of this former elegance can still be seen - just. In 1905 it became a school, when Hazards House school moved from its High Street premises. Calling itself 'Braunstone House, a Day School for Girls and Little Boys' it finally amalgamated with Westmont School and moved to Carisbrooke Mall in the 1940s. Some former pupils still recall their time at Braunstone School. "It was a creepy place and teachers were quite strict," commented one.

The old Braunstone House school is now a toy museum

In the mid-1960s, the place was bought by Mrs Irene (Micky) Smith and her husband Stan, who converted it into an antiques showroom, with workshops behind and living accommodation above. Immediately they moved in, the ghost made itself known to her. Micky has since died, but her sister Margaret and brother-in-law, Alan Wilkins, recall the events well. "It started the very first night they were there. A dark figure appeared at the foot of the bed and stood watching her. She saw it many times after that - usually in the same place in front of the window. Micky felt that the ghost was looking at her, although she never saw his face. She never tried to touch him and was never frightened by the figure," said Alan.

The Puritan Ghost

"The ghost was usually dressed in the same clothes; a long black coat, white shirt and white, Puritan-style collar. He wore long, black knee stockings and there was a black three-corner hat on his dark hair. His face was always unclear for she could never see his features.

"Micky soon got used to having him around and saw the apparition most nights. He would usually appear when she went downstairs to put the milk bottles out at night. There he would stand, on the landing, in the dining room doorway, or at the top of stairs. She would always call out 'Goodnight' to him."

The ghost was seen all over the upper part of the building and one night, when Alan stayed there, he too, saw the figure. "I had gone to bed but wasn't asleep. Looking towards the door I saw a dark shape walking across the room. It came through the door and as I watched, it walked straight through the opposite wall into the next door bedroom. It was a man's figure and it appeared solid. It wasn't completely dark at the time and there was light coming into the room from street lamps. The apparition seemed unaware of me," he added.

Alan recalls that the ghost wore a long, black coat and a three-cornered black hat. He, too, was unable to see its face. He and Margaret agree, "It was an uncomfortable house. There were lots of passageways with steps up and down to rooms; it just felt creepy. You were never really warm there, even in summer. Sometimes a curious whispering could be heard, although you could not make out the words."

A tap on the shoulder

Robin Smith, now of Mill Street, Newport, who lived at Braunstone House with his parents, recalled, "Things started the day we moved in. Mum came downstairs after putting some things away in the attics and told us something strange had just happened. A hand had tapped her on the shoulder and as she turned to see who it was, a figure behind her vanished. She saw it many times after that. A friend of ours who lived with us for a considerable time was terrified one night when she encountered the ghost. She had been sleeping in my sister's room when she woke to see someone in an old-fashioned, long, black cloak and what looked like a feathered hat standing over her. She dived beneath the bedclothes. But when she peered out a few moments later, he was still there!

A ghostly Puritan was seen here

"I never saw anything while I lived in the house, but on several occasions I was woken by a feeling of weight on my bed, as if someone had just sat down on it. There was definitely something there. I pushed against it; it didn't move, but it left an indentation in the bedclothes..."

Subsequent owner, Mrs Carter, who lived at Braunstone House from 1976 until 1998, was relatively untroubled by any lingering presence. "It's a peaceful place now," she insisted. However, shortly after the family moved in, her daughter Lorraine glimpsed a dark figure standing in the corner of her attic bedroom. She also heard a thunderous hammering on the bedroom door. But when she opened it...no one was there.

The Taylor family bought Braunstone House just before Christmas 1998, and the ancient building now enjoys a new lease of life as Timmy Taylor's Toy Box. There, in the former schoolhouse, visitors can take a step back in time to their own childhood and wallow in nostalgia, for Elizabeth Taylor has amassed an incredible collection of toys and ephemera of the 20th century which is on show to the public.

She and her husband Steve are quite accustomed to living among ghosts. They previously ran the nearby haunted Castle Inn, Newport's oldest pub, as well as the former Newport Squash Club, which Elizabeth asserts was home to a disturbing and malign presence.

The Taylors live above the toy museum and are keeping an eye out for the resident ghost, although it has yet to show himself to them. Too busy inspecting the fascinating toys and relics in the museum no doubt!

So who is the faceless phantom haunting Braunstone House? This area of old Newport is something of a supernatural hot spot. The Grey Lady of Woolworth's appears next door, while the Mauve Lady of Lugley Street glides out of a doorway opposite. King Charles I's unhappy phantom lingers at the old Grammar School across the road, while a few doors away, the town's former Oxfam Shop is home to a small, elderly apparition which also wears a three-cornered hat. (Read about them in earlier Ghosts of the Isle of Wight books).

Could Mr Grey, the gentleman for whom the house was originally built, be keeping a watchful eye on his property? Only the ghosts know. And they're not telling.

WHAT LURKS AT LUGLEY HOUSE?

A ghost who goes by the name of 'Albert George' has been heard just across the road at Lugley House, which is one of the finest of Newport's remaining 'town houses'.

Albert George is a cut above most of the other ghosts around here. Not for him are footsteps, creaking, groaning or the rattling of chains so

A ghost called 'Albert George' haunts Lugley House

beloved of traditional phantoms. Certainly not! Albert George plays the organ instead. He was heard practising one night by an ex-policeman when he was working for the finance company, Medens. Former manager, Bob Shepheard, recalls, "He went upstairs into the little fireproof and soundproof room where we stored our records. But returned looking white and shaken.

"At first he was reluctant to talk about what had happened, but finally told of how he had heard the sound of organ music playing upstairs, although he was the only person in the locked building at the time.

"He was a big chap, not easily spooked. He had been a local copper for years and had seen and heard some odd things in his time. He had to confess though, that ghostly organ music was the strangest!"

Although they never saw the ghost materialise, staff at Lugley House referred to him as Albert George. Whenever anything was moved or vanished, he was always blamed.

The building dates mainly from Georgian times and Bob Shepheard recalls that the deep brick-lined cellars with their dark passageways, always felt unnaturally cold and uncomfortable. No one went down there willingly, he said.

Mrs Pettit, office manager for 26 years, knew the building well and agreed that it was a fascinating place. "Staff were well used to tales of the ghost. We would sometimes hear footsteps and the sound of someone moving about upstairs when the place was empty. Some even refused to go upstairs alone and insisted that the attics were haunted. We don't know why he is called Albert George, however, or why his spirit is still attached to the place."

In 1871 it is recorded that the house belonged to Mrs R Pittis, a member of the well-known Newport family of auctioneers, valuers, estate and land agents. Earlier this century it was owned by local solicitor, Alexander Young-James, later becoming a doctor's house with the surgery alongside. During the last war it was leased by the Ministry of Agriculture and later bought by the Christian Science Society. When they moved to nearby Crocker Street, Lugley House was taken over by the finance company Medens.

Now it is the headquarters of the Medina Housing Association, and although Bob Downer, community development manager, hasn't met the ghost himself, he said staff spoke of a presence in the old building. This is usually felt down in those cellars, and one computer operator

Engraving of Newport dated 1842

recently returned to her desk, ashen-faced and trembling, convinced that she had encountered Albert George there.

Other staff are reluctant to go down to the basement, because those who do sometimes feel a tap on the shoulder. But, when they turn round, they are always alone…

Chapter Nine

FAVOURITE HAUNTS

THE WELCOMING GHOST

When Sylvia and Ray Porter moved into their new home at Lushington Hill, Wootton, they discovered there was something missing from the estate agent's particulars. He had omitted to mention that a ghost in a tricorn hat and riding boots would be waiting to greet them!

The couple, who now live at Newport Road, Cowes, had bought the old house in 1979 and moved in on June 1 that year. "Everything was in a muddle. I was running up and down the stairs with boxes and packing cases when I saw him," said Sylvia.

"A tall man dressed in black was standing in the corner of the landing. I thought at first it was Ray, but on closer inspection I could see it was a figure wearing a three-cornered hat, a long, thick, caped coat and riding boots with the tops turned down.

"His face was not visible and I couldn't see his feet at all, for as I stared at him, he started to disappear.... from the ground upwards. I think I had surprised him. At first it didn't register that I had met a ghost. I just put it down to the stress of moving and thought it was a figment of my imagination, particularly as I was in a bit of a state because my father had died suddenly that day. I certainly didn't say a word to Ray about what I had seen," Sylvia insisted.

The next evening when they were still hard at work sorting through packing cases, Ray went upstairs with an armful of belongings.

"He came downstairs a few moments later and announced, 'We have got a ghost!' I turned round and said, 'Yes I know; I saw it yesterday. I wonder if it is the same one?' We compared descriptions and decided that it was the very same ghost. He had been wearing that costume and standing in the same place on the landing. We nicknamed him Fred."

Sylvia and Ray never actually saw Fred again, although they could usually tell when he was around. He was obviously an inquisitive ghost and liked to know when something new was happening or if someone was visiting - like the time Sylvia's in-laws came to stay one Christmas.

"They had the spare bedroom and one day when I was in the dining room, which is directly underneath, I heard the sound of heavy footsteps crossing the empty room overhead. I shouted to Ray, 'Fred's upstairs' and we both ran up to look - but the room was empty."

Another time Fred made his ghostly presence felt, Sylvia was sitting in the bay window of the lounge; Ray was relaxing on the other side of the room. "Out of the corner of my eye I saw something move, then the cushion on the chair next to mine flattened as if someone had sat down. Although I could see nothing there, I stared hard at where Fred's head would have been and then I noticed the plant near the chair moving..... as if someone had just brushed past it."

Sylvia and Ray subsequently sold the house to a middle-aged couple, and now live at Cowes. "The previous owners never told us about Fred, so we didn't mention the ghost to the new people. He does seem to be attached to the house, but he was very quiet for the last few years we lived there. Maybe he has moved on."

THE GHOSTLY CUPPA

Whatever haunts the Culver Lodge Hotel in Sandown still likes to make an occasional cuppa, for since hoteliers Peter and Anne LeLievre took over the 20-bedroom hotel in 1988, they have often found their electric kettle in the kitchen switched on when no-one has been there.

On one occasion when they were both standing in the kitchen talking to a member of staff, something walked noisily across a metal grating outside the kitchen door, the kettle was switched on, then the teapot suddenly fell off a shelf at on the other side of the room.

"He didn't get his cup of tea that day," laughed Peter. "Those unseen footsteps and the switching on of the kettle happened so often that we took no notice after a while."

However, on one summer's evening in

A 1952 advertisement for Culver Lodge

1992, when Peter saw an elderly ghost moving between ground floor rooms at about 9pm, he was not quite so blasé.

Although the figure was only visible for a few brief moments, Peter clearly remembers, "It was a man about 5ft 6ins tall with an arched or humped back; the sort of curvature of the spine an elderly person would have. The ghost emerged from what is now our games room and walked across the passageway into another room. I have to confess I could not bring myself to follow it. I turned straight for the bar - and stayed there."

Peter could not see the ghost's features or distinguish details of clothing. "It was not quite solid, but a light, greyish figure, all one colour; a creamy-grey. It is very difficult to find the right way to describe it. This is certainly something I will not forget in a hurry. It really shook me."

A GENTLE SOUL....

A ghost carrying a ladder appeared to a very startled guest at another Sandown hotel one night in May 1995. A school party from the mainland, with several accompanying teachers, had been staying for a week at The Lawns Hotel on the Broadway, when the curious incident occurred.

Tom Collins who ran the hotel until 1999, with wife Hazel, daughter Angela, and her husband Adrian, said that while chatting to one of the teachers, he asked if everything was OK.

"She said it was, then asked if we knew we had a ghost in the hotel. She told me she had seen it the previous night in a ground floor corridor. It had been carrying a ladder, and at first she thought it was me coming to do some emergency maintenance work. The teacher had left her door open so that she could hear the children in case there was a problem. The figure, still carrying its ladder, walked up to her bedroom door, came inside, then vanished."

This corridor is in the old kitchen area of the hotel, which was originally built as a Victorian home. After Tom and his family bought The Lawns in 1990, the frequency of strange happenings there increased. The first manifestation they noticed was a strong smell of beer in the first floor hallway, which seemed to come and go for no reason. Guests started to report lights being switched on and off in one of the bedrooms. In this same room, another guest claimed someone kept trying to open the door - although whenever she looked out, there was no one there.

A ghost carrying a ladder was seen at this hotel

She could actually see the door being physically pushed, the guest told Tom.

In 1993, one visitor saw a ghostly figure walking along the landing while other guests noticed cold spots in their rooms. Doors in the kitchen flew violently open as Tom was clearing up one night, and when Adrian's father was staying at The Lawns, a ghostly shape tried to materialize in front of him. As this figure began to form at the top of the stairs, Adrian's father clamped his eyes tightly shut and refused to look again until he was sure it had disappeared.

Downstairs in the large, comfy lounge, another guest told Hazel she had been watching the television when an arrangement of dried flowers on the table in front of her started to move. As she watched in fascination, invisible ghostly fingers actually squeezed the flower heads, knocking petals onto the table.

Whoever the ghostly handyman with the ladder is, he enjoys the occasional smoke while listening to music. Sometimes the radio in the bar comes on of its own accord, and Hazel smells the strong and distinctive whiff of tobacco smoke at the dead of night in the bedroom. Usually it is cigarette smoke, but occasionally the more pungent smell of old-fashioned pipe tobacco can be detected.

In June 1999, Tom and Hazel sold the hotel to Barbara Mace, who now runs The Lawns with her family. The hotel ghost is now so well-known that guests often ask after it, and although Barbara has not seen anything yet, she has felt its presence.

"I was alone and ironing in the kitchen one day when I sensed there was someone in the room with me. It was quite calm and I wasn't at all frightened. I knew there was a gentle soul watching me. It was really rather nice," she said.

THE HARTLAND LADY

In the nearby holiday resort of Shanklin, the shade of an elderly lady who couldn't bear to leave her old home, liked to keep an eye on things at the Hartland Hotel in Victoria Avenue. The hotel's authentic Victorian-themed restaurant must have raised the ghost's spirits when it was opened by Jenny Lever, who ran the Hartland for 27 years with her former husband.

"We called her 'The Lady' after we discovered that she had actually lived there with her son many years earlier, and had so loved the place that her spirit returned after death," said Jenny. "I got on well with her. She was quite friendly and very interested in all the alterations we made to the hotel, which was called the Hartland Guest House when we bought it. She wasn't much trouble, although she did move a few things around and it was embarrassing when guests asked us who the elderly lady in the old-fashioned clothes was." 'The Lady' who

HARTLAND GUEST HOUSE
VICTORIA AVENUE   Telephone 2563   SHANKLIN

Separate Tables in Dining Room

18-Hole Putting Course

Covered Verandah

TERMS:
(Fully inclusive— no extras)
4½ to 7 gns.

Delightfully situated in own grounds, within 10 minutes walk of Sea, Old Village and Chine. H. & C., Reading Lights, and Interior Sprung Mattresses in all Bedrooms. Gas or Electric Fires available. Comfortable Lounge and Smokeroom. Good Food

Illustrated Brochure on request   Resident Proprietors: F./Lieut. and Mrs. F. BADHAM

A 1950s advertisement for the Hartland Guest House

wore a long black skirt and blouse, usually carried a Bible, while a smaller book hung from a chain at her waist. She was often accompanied by two little phantom cats, which would set Jenny's two dogs barking wildly as they silently followed their ghostly mistress.

One visitor who had spent her honeymoon at the Hartland many years earlier, recalled a very old lady who had lived with the family. This guest was able to describe the old lady's cats and the book she wore on a chain.

Soon after taking over the Hartland, Jenny consulted a local medium to see if she could move the elderly ghost on. "She advised me to write on a piece of paper who we were and what we were planning to do to her former home and to leave this under a lighted candle," said Jenny.

The Hartland Hotel, Shanklin, is haunted by the ghost of a former owner

Clearly reassured by this, 'The Lady' vanished for a year, but returned when Jenny and her husband started to make alterations to the hotel, knocking walls down and installing bathrooms. The ghost made her presence known in one particular bedroom, which Jenny later learned had been hers. As well as keeping an eye on her old home 'The Lady' also watched over Jenny and her family. One day when Jenny's husband was drilling into a kitchen wall, the ghost appeared at his side, just in time to warn that he was about to cut through the cooker cable!

Lesley and Steve Hall bought the Hartland Hotel, with its Victorian restaurant, in 1992. Although they were aware of its haunted reputation, neither of them saw 'The Lady' although staff still spoke of seeing her.

The hotel was sold to the Woodward family in 1994 and is now run by Diana Woodward-Parker and her husband Dan. "We have heard that the hotel is haunted but have never seen anything ourselves," said Diana. "As we have made a number of alterations to the place; I only hope this means that 'The Lady' approves of what we have done."

Chapter Ten

WATERY GRAVES

LOST ON THE TITANIC

Nineteen Hundred and Twelve looked set to be a very good year for William Cheverton. One of ten children, William who lived with his parents, William senior and Emma, at Mill Street, Newport, had joined the merchant navy when he left school and travelled the world. Now aged 27, he was engaged to be married to his sweetheart.

William had worked his way up to become a First Class saloon steward with the White Star Line, sailing regularly out of Southampton on the ocean-going liners. In April 1912, William was offered a highly desirable job - the chance to serve on the largest and finest steamer in the world........the RMS Titanic.

Titanic sailed from Southampton at noon on Wednesday, 7 April. Crowds lined the waterfront, and as she passed the Isle of Wight, many local people watched her stately progress. She was eleven storeys high, a sixth of a mile long and carried 2,207 passengers and crew. Most of the crew came from Southampton, but a few were from the Island.

When the Titanic called at Queenstown, where many young Irish emigrants boarded, bound for a new life in America, William Cheverton posted a letter to his parents. He wrote telling them of the excellent voyage and his hopes of doing well, especially on the return trip when a very large list of American passengers was booked - and he had expectations of some exceedingly good tips.

At 11.40pm on Sunday, 11 April, Titanic struck the iceberg. There were no bells or sirens, no general alarm. Stewards, William Cheverton among them, went from cabin to cabin rousing their sleepy First Class passengers, coaxing them into lifejackets and helping them to the lifeboats.

The rest, as we know, is history. The Isle of Wight County Press summed up the tragedy on page 8 with the headline: **APPALLING SHIPPING DISASTER, LARGEST LINER SUNK, LOSS OF OVER 1500 LIVES, ISLANDERS IN DEATH ROLL.**

A number of local crew members were listed as dead or missing.

There were seven stewards, one stewardess, and a fireman. Two others from Ryde, Quartermaster Walter John Perkis, and newly-married Second Steward G. Wheat, aged 32, were saved. Quartermaster Perkis, 36, was given charge of Lifeboat 4, which launched from the Titanic's port side at 1.50am with just 34 passengers. It could have carried 65.

William Cheverton, who died on the Titanic

The Cheverton family waited anxiously for news of William's fate, but it wasn't until two months later that his body was recovered from those icy waters. It was 370 miles from the spot where Titanic sank. His was body number 334 and he was found with two fellow Islanders who were Titanic stewards. But no memorial marks his final resting-place. All three bodies were hastily returned to the sea. His heartbroken parents, Emma and William, were unable to claim or bury the body of their eldest son. Neither was poor William's spirit able to rest easy until his last wishes had been respected.

His favourite sister was known affectionately as 'Little Nell' as the 29-year-old was crippled and had been born a dwarf. As she would never marry or be able to support herself, William had promised always to look after her. From his earnings of £2 9s a week, he sent his mother at least £18 a year for his sister's keep.

The Titanic's wealthy owners offered just £54 for William's loss. The Judge at Newport County Court, however, ordered the White Star Line to pay maximum compensation of £300. The case went to the Court of Appeal where three judges dismissed the shipping line's appeal and William's sister finally got the money. Perhaps his spirit was able to find peace at last.

William's great-nephew, John Smith, now retired, lives in Wootton. As a lad he was fascinated to see family mementoes and to hear tales of how the Titanic was lost. John remembers meeting most of William's brothers and sisters, Tom, Edward, Florence, Alice, Lillian, Nell, Clara, Dorothy and Emma.

In 1912, while William was away at sea, Lillian, John's grandmother, was due to marry her sweetheart, a soldier in the Royal Suffolk Regiment stationed at Albany. Sadly he was killed in Flanders in March 1918, a month before John's father was born in the Cheverton family home in Mill Street.

*Author's note: The Oscar-winning movie 'Titanic' renewed public interest in the disaster, which has over the years been the subject of many books and films. Among them is a novel called 'Futility' by struggling author Morgan Robertson. His story tells of a gigantic liner, the Titan, the largest ship ever built which, loaded with rich, complacent people, was wrecked on an iceberg one cold April night. Hardly a new idea for a novel you might think, however, Robertson's book was published in 1898, **fourteen years** before Titanic went down on her maiden voyage. So where did Robertson get the idea for his story? Was it a premonition?*

PREMONITION OR DREAM?

Premonitions, precognition, dreams. Where do they come from? Are they glimpses of the future? If so, should we heed them?

A gang of labourers working on a new harbour wall at Newport Quay on 14 April 1907, had every reason to be thankful that their boss, Mr Williams, a Newport builder, acted on his dream. Mr Williams had won the tender to extend the new harbour wall for Newport Corporation for the princely sum of £166. Work between tides was going well and with the help of a steam crane, the new 16-foot high wall was underway. Its foundations firmly bedded into the riverbed, the solid concrete wall was five foot thick at the base. Mud and clay excavated from the river in front of the wall was used to fill in the vacant space behind.

On the morning of April 14, Mr Williams woke with a start, his heart pounding. He had been dreaming, and his dreams had not been sweet. That massive wall, his pride and joy, was slipping into the river. As it split open, the huge chunks of concrete fell on top of his men, killing them as they scrambled in vain to get out of the way.

Telling himself it was only a nightmare, probably the result of that extra glass of port the night before, Mr Williams hurried to the quay to check that all was well. It was. The wall was intact and in the cold light of day he felt foolish. But as the day wore on and as work proceeded he grew more and more uneasy. Mr Williams called a halt to the work and inspected the wall once again. Ominous cracks suddenly started to appear; by 3pm astonished labourers could only stand and watch as the wall collapsed into the river.

No one was injured as some 150 feet of the wall broke up and slid into the river. It was the pressure caused by the weight of the mud and clay

Did a premonition prevent disaster when this harbour wall collapsed in 1907?

being dumped behind the wall which caused its collapse. The sight of those huge pieces of concrete sticking out of the mud was a nine-day wonder, attracting the local townsfolk in large numbers. But for his nightmare, Mr Williams knew his men would have been killed when that wall fell. He even told the Isle of Wight County Press newspaper, which carried a report of the premonition or dream.

THE CURSE OF DODNOR...

Those who have died violently at the hand of another are the unruly dead; people or spirits who live in a limbo of their own, in some state between life and death, restless, dissatisfied, longing for release. They murmur, they mourn themselves and what might have been. They whisper the names of their attackers, those men and women who still walk the earth, unknown, unaccused, unpunished and unrepentant.

Across the River Medina at Dodnor, the place is cursed, it is said. The origins of this malediction are unknown, but a surprising number of people who linger there seem to meet an untimely end. The Curse of Dodnor appears to have claimed a remarkable number of lives over the past two centuries and I am grateful to Newport Harbourmaster, Wayne Pritchett, for the information:

In 1799, 33-year-old churchman William Tate was found dead in a field at Dodner (as it was then known) while trudging through deep snow to take food to a family cut off by the bad weather. Although he was on an errand of mercy, death was caused by a blow to the head......was it accident or murder?

In July 1826, two Newport carriers, George Mundell, 22, and George Knowles, 21, were transporting gunpowder from a barge beached at Dodnor Hard, to the Barracks at Parkhurst. Going up Dodnor Lane, the gunpowder exploded, killing both men instantly. Two horses also died and two soldiers escorting the explosive, died later in hospital.

The River Medina at Dodnor, looking towards Newport

In November 1864, David Jones, 35, a labourer at the cement mills, drowned when a freak squall overturned his sailing dinghy as he passed Dodnor on his way home from work.

The following year, in April 1865, a young Shide woman, Edith Way, went for a Sunday afternoon walk along the riverbank. Her body was later found in a ditch near Broken Bridge at Hurstake, Dodnor. She had drowned, although there were just a few inches of water in the ditch.

In December the same year, Thomas Rogers, a 60-year-old lighterman from Little London, Newport, fell from a lighter as it was towed past Dodnor at night. Did he fall....or was he pushed by an unseen hand?

Newport Harbour in the early 20th century

In 1872, 14-year-old Frank Lambert drowned at Dodnor when a dinghy he had hired from Newport capsized, one calm August day.

In April 1891, Captain William Pengilly, 43, master of the Queen of the South, which was berthed at the cement mills, just south of Dodnor, fell from the railway viaduct and drowned in the millpond on his way back from Newport, one night.

In the year 1898, the river claimed two young lives in separate accidents near Dodnor. In August, Arthur Caudrey, 18, and a friend went out in a dinghy one hot afternoon. Foolishly, although he could not swim, Caudrey went into the water. Unable to get back to the boat, he drowned. The inquest jury, which heard that the body of this "promising young man" was pulled ashore at Hurstake, returned a verdict of accidental drowning.

September 1898, saw the year's second tragic accident opposite Dodnor, when 14-year-old Clara Pragnell drowned as the dinghy she was riding in capsized. Young Clara, a nursemaid, lived at Dodnor and was the daughter of the night watchman at the cement mill. She was in the boat with her mother and younger sister Annie returning from Cowes Carnival, one glorious moonlight night at 11pm. The boat hit a tidal whirlpool and all the passengers were pitched into the seething water. Clara's body was recovered six hours later by her distraught father, who found her floating in the dark, muddy water at Dodnor.

The new century opened with the death of Edmund Matthews, a 29-year-old Pearl Insurance Agent who, in June 1900, stole a dinghy from Newport and committed suicide at Dodnor.

In February 1906, Captain John Whiting, master of the vessel Glendevon, berthed at the cement mills, fell from the Dodnor railway viaduct while returning to his ship at night. He later died from his injuries.

In 1921, Alf Sheaf, landlord of the Ship and Launch, at Hurstake, Dodnor, drowned after falling from the boat which he used to commute to and from his pub - for the little inn could not be reached by road. His cries for help were apparently mistaken for ducks squawking!

More recently, Toby Sheaf, a well-known big yacht skipper, merchant seaman and fisherman, was found dead in his dinghy, drifting at Dodnor, by the crew of a Mew Langton barge.

In June 1989, a young man was killed at Dodnor in a bizarre accident. He fell from his small powerboat, which then did a U-turn and ran him over as he tried to swim ashore. One of the witnesses to this incident was also drowned five years later....while on his way home to Dodnor.

A STRANGE FIGURE

Old Herbie Young, a storeman who lived at the Hurstake Inn at Dodnor, met a ghost one night in Dodnor Lane.

As an elderly man wearing a long coat, high-collared shirt and top hat, came towards him, Herbie said, "Good Evening" but the gentleman didn't reply and walked past him. As Herbie turned to look again at the strange figure, it vanished into thin air.

Another local man, Sid Mew, who now lives at Pan, met the same ghost one night in 1963. He had been out courting and was on his way home at 11.15pm when, he too, saw that figure wearing a long coat with a high collar and a three-quarter height top hat, moving towards him.

Sid realised that although they were both on a gravel track, the man's footsteps made no sound. When they were a yard or so apart Sid called out "Goodnight Mate." He got no reply. The figure had vanished.

"I got down that lane a bit quick after that," admits Sid.

Who was this tall elderly ghost in the top hat? No one knows. It was seen on both occasions close to the old Workhouse Cemetery in Dodnor Lane. Obviously a well-to-do gentleman, was he a doctor or overseer from the House of Industry? Many a poor soul lived and died in the

A view of the River Medina and Dodnor in the early 20th Century

workhouse. Parts of the building which date back to 1773 can still be seen at St Mary's Hospital, and stories are told of hauntings there too. (Read about them in Ghosts of the IW Book III)

Chapter Eleven

RYDE'S MOST HAUNTED HOUSE

St John's Park at Ryde was an exclusive Victorian residential development. An up-market suburban housing estate for the gentry, it was built between 1854 and 1862 on what was once St John's estate, belonging to the Simeon family.

Named after St John's in Newfoundland, the estate remained intact only until the mid-1800s, when much of it was sold off. More than thirty prestigious villas were built there on an irregular, teardrop-shaped portion of land fronting Easthill and Westhill Roads. Keyholders enjoyed access to the private park and gardens behind their homes, which once boasted two tennis courts, a bandstand and formal walks lined with shrubs and trees.

This once-splendid park was, however, swallowed by the expanding town of Ryde. Today, few of the imposing three and four-storey properties are family homes; the majority have been converted into flats or demolished and the sites redeveloped.

One of these large houses on the inner side of St John's Park was divided into nine flats in the 1940s. The house, complete with basement servants' quarters and attic nurseries, was built originally for a doctor, but later became the home of General Adolphe Zelaziewitch, and subsequently that of Major General Charles Fanshawe and his family.

Otherwise, little is known of its history or why it is so haunted. Early maps show the area was once known as Troublefeild (1608) and Trouble Fields (1812) ....a portent of things to come?

I have not revealed the exact location of the house for reasons which should become obvious.

GHOSTLY WINGBEATS

As newlyweds, John and Margaret Oakley moved into the top floor flat of the rambling old house in 1965. They were excited to have a little place of their own, but that delight was clouded when, over the next six years, a series of strange but seemingly unconnected incidents occurred there. The couple now live in York Avenue, East Cowes, and John admits that for several years after they left that flat, he experienced unpleasant and recurring dreams about it.

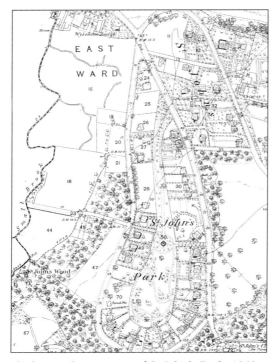

Ordnance Survey map of St John's Park, 1862

"Everything was fine at first. We were just married and taken up with each other. But then I became increasingly uneasy living there and conscious of an unwelcoming atmosphere."

The first odd happening took place the very first night, when John switched off the bedside light, and it immediately came on again, by itself. Then, in the living room one Sunday afternoon, John and Margaret let their pet budgerigars fly loose around the room, having put the birds' huge cage squarely in the middle of the table. Suddenly, the empty cage rose into the air and then tilted forward with such force that it would have fallen to the floor if a chair had not been in the way.

The next odd event was some months later when, hearing a huge crash from the kitchen, John rushed in to find all the saucepans and baking tins which were kept on the mantelpiece, lying across the room.

When Margaret was in the kitchen one day, she watched as a matchbox started to move end over end across the top of their twin-tub washing machine (which was not switched on at the time). Then the cups hanging from hooks on the kitchen dresser started to swing - one at a time until they were all moving together quite violently.

Just before Christmas one year, John recalls that the ornamental glass tree decorations, which had been hung around the picture rail in the living room, started to swing about wildly as if being shaken by invisible hands. Although a carpet covered the entire floor in the living room, Margaret heard the sound of a toddler's or small child's footsteps running on a wooden floor in the room with her.

Occasionally that room would grow unnaturally cold, and small items would disappear, usually turning up again later. Not so Margaret's engagement and eternity rings, alas. Both vanished without trace in the flat, never to be seen again.

An old dumb waiter hatch was used as an alcove for ornaments. Pride of place went to a musical box which, one day, started to play on its own, although no-one had wound it nor lifted the lid to set it going. "It frightened the life out of us, yet when we opened it to make it play again, it wouldn't work," said Margaret.

For a while her parents came to live with the young couple. Margaret's father, who worked night shifts, was in the flat alone one day when he felt an urge to look towards the hall window. There, watching him was the apparition of a young girl.

But the worst experience the young couple had in that flat, once part of the nursery to the old house, came in the early hours of the morning when both were sound asleep. "We were suddenly woken by what sounded like a giant pair of wings flapping over the bed. It was so loud that I put the light on and it stopped immediately. The sensation was in the room almost all round us. It made an incredible sound and was so close," recalled John with a shudder.

"It was horrible and it took us quite a while to get back to sleep again. The next night we lay there dreading it would happen again. It did. But as soon as I put the light on, the wingbeats stopped. We didn't get much sleep that night either, and a few days later we moved out of the flat."

TWENTY YEARS LATER.....

That flat was still haunted almost twenty years later in 1992, when Georgina and Dean Rogers moved in. They, however, quickly became used to a gentle, almost comforting presence which was very protective of their newborn baby.

The couple and their baby son, Connor, often heard a woman's footsteps walking around the flat. Usually the footsteps would start pacing between 11pm and midnight. A heavy fire door would open and close, and occasionally a reflection of 'something indefinable' could be glimpsed in the windows.

"It was very quiet here at night, you could hear the presence moving around. If we had guests, she was particularly active and seemed to want to see who they were." When Georgina's brother, John, spent a night on the sofa in the lounge, he awoke to find the unseen woman was lifting his arm, while at the same time he could feel breath on his neck. Although the sofa was pushed back against the wall, the faint outline of a bricked-up doorway is just visible there, and it was from this direction that the ghost's breathing was coming.

Bars on the windows with unusual ornamental locks and catches are a reminder of the days when the top floor flat was once the nursery. Whatever walked there was particularly attracted to young Connor, for early one morning, Georgina heard those footsteps moving about. They stopped at Connor's cot and he suddenly woke. Then Georgina heard a woman's voice soothing the baby. "Shhhhhh, shhhhhh" came the soft whisper.

Dean and Georgina are convinced that the ghost in their flat was that of a nurse or nanny, who would have had charge of the nursery. "I was often aware of her when I was looking after Connor, feeding him or changing his nappy. Many times I felt a finger tap me on the shoulder, but when I turned round there would be no one there," said Georgina.

"One day when Connor was teething, I heard a banging noise in the kitchen and went in to find his special teething biscuits had been taken out of the cupboard and were out on the worktop ready for him. On another occasion when Connor was being naughty, I got cross and shouted at him.

"Suddenly, a heavy cookery book was lifted from its shelf and banged down, hard, as if to say 'Stop it'. I apologised and said sorry. The ghost would become agitated if I was annoyed with the baby.

"I would find myself talking to her. Often when I was changing a nappy or feeding Connor, I could feel her looking over my shoulder to make sure I was doing things correctly. She was wonderful to have there, very reassuring. I believe she loved children and approved of us because of Connor."

Georgina discovered that she was expecting the baby shortly after she and Dean moved into the flat. Soon after Connor was born, the ghostly nanny could be heard moving about the flat in the early hours, checking on the baby and if he woke, she would be there soothing him back to sleep.

One night the baby woke and Dean got up to see to him but, before he could do anything, the unseen presence was quickly there with the child. Dean stood in the doorway, listening, as that soothing voice whispered "Shhhh, shhhhh".

Ghosts were everywhere

"Although we were very happy in our flat, we were aware that other tenants in the house were having problems," said Georgina. "We noticed that in some of the downstairs flats, people didn't stay there long and they were often empty. We would sometimes see a couple from the ground floor flat, Ed and Madge Paige, sitting in the garden in their nightclothes because they were too scared to go back to bed. There seemed to be ghosts everywhere. You would sometimes feel them around you in the very fabric of the building, brushing against you as you went up and down the stairs.

"Supernatural activity there seemed centred around that ground floor flat and the basement one below. They were the worst. One girl who moved into the basement with her children called in a priest to have it exorcised, while another couple who went to view the Paige's vacant flat, ran screaming from the place. They had heard a deep, menacing chuckle coming from the fireplace in the living room, the shaken pair insisted."

But Dean and Georgina were untroubled by any such malevolence in their top floor flat. Even before they moved in, they were the ghostly nanny's chosen tenants it seems. Georgina explained, "When we went to view the flat we had arranged to meet the landlord there. He hurried to greet us but said that unfortunately he had been given the wrong key and could not let us in. He appeared all hot and bothered, and rushed off, saying he would arrange to meet us another day with the correct key. He had left the other one under the mat and we could try it for ourselves if we wanted.

"We went upstairs and put the key in the lock. It turned first time and we went in. The flat was gorgeous. We knew immediately it was for us. The rooms were huge, light and airy. The place was perfect; we had to have it. Outside on the landing we shut the door and Dean checked it was locked. I wondered why the landlord had any difficulty with the key and tried it once more. It wouldn't even fit into the lock, let alone turn. Yet we had opened the door with it!"

The family left the flat in 1995 when Georgina was expecting her second child. The thought of four flights of stairs with two children was too daunting, and they moved to Green Street in Ryde. But their legacy from that flat was a £400 electricity bill, most of which was run up by the ghost. "The bill for just three months came to over £400," said Georgina. "We asked Southern Electric to check the meter as it was so incredibly high. They insisted it was correct, so one night we turned everything in the flat off and watched the meter. It did not move. But as soon as the ghost started her nightly wanderings, the meter started to spin round even though we were not using any electricity.

"The electricity company did not believe us of course, and the last few months we were in the flat she was very active and ran us up a large bill. We have only just finished paying it off in instalments," said Georgina.

"I was very sorry to leave her. I almost wish we could have taken the ghost with us when we moved. I always felt that no harm could come to Connor when she was watching over him. But with such high electric bills, it would have been cheaper to have had a real live nanny!"

THE ADMIRAL'S GHOST

In the basement flat at the other end of the building, Moira lived with her father Bill for 32 years until his death in 1993. Although she agreed to talk of their experiences, Moira is reluctant to be identified, so I have not used their real names.

Moira, who now lives on a farm in West Sussex, moved into the basement flat when she was twenty-one. The flat was once servants' quarters and part of the wine cellar, while their living room was formerly the billiard room. In all the time she lived there, Moira never saw any of the ghosts herself, although Bill met them on numerous occasions. He was most familiar with an apparition he called 'The Admiral'.

This spectral sailor appeared in the living room, just five feet away from where Bill was sitting. 'The Admiral' wore a jacket or tunic with brass buttons and gold braid on the shoulders, knee-length breeches with hose. His shoes were buckled and on his head was a tricorn hat.

"He appeared to be quite solid and stood there without speaking for quite a while before he faded away. Curiously Dad never saw his face - there was just a blank where it should have been. Dad saw him many times over the years and the sightings seemed to go in cycles. He would put in several appearances over a few months and then it could be as long as four or five years before he returned. And when this ghost appeared, others would follow soon afterwards."

Bill could see some of the house's other long-dead occupants, ghostly gardeners working in the grounds, and other apparitions in Victorian costumes on the front porch. Whether they were visitors or servants, he was never sure. He also glimpsed apparitions who appeared to be sitting in a waiting room. One day, as he watched, a lady in ankle-length skirts stood up. She carried a baby which was wearing a little white lace bonnet. Both disappeared through a wall into what is now a front ground floor flat.

Although Moira never met the ghosts herself, she was sometimes aware of their presence. The flat would sometimes grow unnaturally cold, lights would be switched off and on by unseen hands and doors would open and close.

"I wasn't worried by all this, I just took it for granted after a while," she said. "We would be in the living room and the door handle would turn. The door would open two or three inches and then it would close again. A few seconds later, the door on the other side of the room would open slightly and then slowly close, as though someone.... or something had just passed through."

ODD AND UNCOMFORTABLE

Louise Pinks who shared the largest flat at the old house for seven months in 1993, found it an odd and uncomfortable place to live.

"It was like someone was always playing games with us. Items of clothing would be moved about and silly things like drawer liners disappeared. It is a strange house. I used to spend a lot of time wandering about the building and it seemed as if the house did not like it. There was a continual feeling of an unseen presence watching me and following me. I hated the place at night and was very glad to move out."

The only time Louise actually saw any ghosts appear was one afternoon in late summer when she

Did a ghostly game of croquet take place here?

witnessed a ghostly game of croquet taking place on the rear lawns.

As she watched in amazement, Louise saw four or five ladies in what appeared to be long, pastel-coloured Victorian costumes, with croquet mallets, who were engrossed in their game. This event from the past lasted just a few short seconds before the verdant lawn with its croquet hoops and the elegant chattering figures reverted to the unkempt back garden once more.

Louise, who works for ferry operators Wightlink, now lives just a few doors away from her former flat in a similar old, but unhaunted house. She keeps an eye on the comings and goings there, and confirms that most people don't tend to stay there for long.

IT'S AN EVIL PLACE

Events in the ground floor flat occupied by Ed and Madge Paige between 1992 and 1993, reached such a level that the terrified couple hurriedly moved out after just a year there. Increasingly weird encounters with the supernatural were just too much for them and Shep, their 12-year-old black and white Labrador, to take.

"Many nights we ended up walking the streets in the early hours because we couldn't bear to be in the flat," said Ed. "One morning we walked round Appley Park at 4am, too frightened to go home."

The couple moved into the flat on 21 June, 1992. At first they were happy there, but then the noises started. Whispering, low murmurs of conversation, footsteps, and conversely 'dead' spots in the hall where all sound seemed to be blanked out or absorbed.

Both Ed and Madge felt the touch of a little ghost dog brushing against their legs. Shep's gaze would often follow the invisible presence to the corner of the room where the cushion on an empty chair would feel warm to the touch - as if it had just been vacated by a small dog. On one occasion Shep went to jump onto the chair and stopped suddenly, licking the apparently empty air.

Then one night when Ed was talking on the phone, the ghostly dog suddenly appeared. A little black and white terrier walked past him into the lounge and vanished. Both Ed and Madge on separate occasions saw a large black shadow hovering in the doorway to the lounge. Madge was just about to start vacuuming one day when she noticed a dense, black oblong shadow drifting from the lounge doorway into the hall - the same area where sound was sometimes blanked out and where she heard voices whispering. "There was a low whisper which stopped when I moved out past the archway. If I stepped back I could hear it again," she said.

In the bedroom Madge felt a cold breeze across her face when she was making the bed. On another occasion she came running out in fright. The temperature had fallen so sharply that she could see her breath in the icy atmosphere. Sudden changes in temperature plagued Ed and Madge during their increasingly uncomfortable year in that flat. One day the living room felt icy cold and the thermometer showed the temperature was zero degrees, within five minutes it had climbed back to 60 degrees again.

At 2am one morning, Ed heard the bedside cupboard drawer open and close although Madge was at his side, fast asleep. "Sometimes it was impossible to sleep. There seemed to be something in the room with us, a presence; it was very uncomfortable, like a pressure building. Shep felt it too and he was on edge and nervy."

Another day, Madge couldn't find her favourite old necklace. It was always kept in her jewellery box. When it did finally turn up, at the bottom of a drawer in the bedroom unit, it was in several pieces.

Neighbours upstairs left in a hurry. Although the flat was unoccupied and unfurnished, but for fitted carpets, Ed and Madge heard the sounds of heavy furniture being moved across the bare wooden floor overhead. "This went on for as long as ten minutes at a stretch. It was terrible. It sounded as if someone was dragging a piano and three piece suite about the place; it happened quite regularly," said Ed.

Determined to get to the bottom of the strange goings-on in their flat, he decided to try and capture the noises on tape. "We went to bed at 1.30am and left the tape recorder in the hall. The next morning there was not a sound on it, not even the noise Shep makes moving about during the night. The following night we tried again. As I have worked with tapes and music all my life I treble checked it to make sure it was working, but next morning the tape was blank again."

After that, Ed tried leaving the recorder overnight in the lounge. This time he was successful. Between 2.30am and 3.30am the tape picked up the sound of two voices. The woman's voice was indistinct and later faded completely from the tape, but the man's voice could be heard calling 'Shep' and saying, 'He's gone over'.

Using noise-activated recorders, local paranormal investigators, Blake Nixon and Stuart Fleming also managed to register the sound of

Ryde, from St John's Park, in an engraving dated 1843

footsteps and voices on tape at the flat. Shortly after this, Ed and Madge moved out, unable to stand the increasing sense that something awful was about to happen.

It was wrecking our health...

"We couldn't live there any longer. It was wrecking our health and turning us all into nervous wrecks - even Shep. Thinking back, nothing ever lived there long. Flies, spiders and other insects always dropped dead and we were forever clearing the remains away."

Lights around the flat would be switched off and on at will by unseen hands, and when the electricity bill arrived it was so impossibly high that Southern Electric ordered a meter check to see where the power was going.

The telephone too, gave trouble, malfunctioning without cause. A BT engineer checked the line but could find no apparent fault. Even the television regularly gave problems. At first Ed and Madge thought it was caused by weather conditions. Later they realised that individual channels were being regularly wiped out by 'something' in their flat.

Traumas of Westhill

Seven years after leaving the flat, Ed is still troubled by events there and feels they may well have caused the sudden decline in Madge's health and her subsequent death.

He kept a detailed record of supernatural happenings at the flat in a diary 'Traumas of Westhill' and has given permission for some extracts to be published here:

August 12th: As I placed my head on the pillow, I heard a baby's distinctive cry coming from the small wardrobe by the window. I got out of bed and opened it. The cry came from the top left-hand side of the wardrobe. I felt it and it appeared to be warm. From that night on I would often hear a baby's cries coming from that wardrobe.

August 15th: I had a vision during the night. In it I saw the whole building in its entirety not long after it was built. It was a magnificent building with its own ballroom, billiards room, wine cellar, kitchens and living quarters.

August 22nd: I was going through some photographs and a very strange thing happened. The people in the photographs began to fade until the picture became a negative. It was a scary experience to watch.

March 19th: We had a visit from Mrs Edgerly, the owner's secretary. She asked if she could leave the keys with us for anyone wishing to rent the flat directly above us. Not long after she left we heard heavy furniture moving about. The furniture appeared to be dragged across an uncarpeted floor. I went outside and could see the flat was in complete darkness. Returning to our flat, the furniture was still being moved about. Next morning we went up to the flat. The room above us was carpeted in thick pile and there wasn't a piece of furniture in the place.

April 12th: This was a terrible night. Shep was restless as was Madge. I knew there was something with us in the bedroom. I felt my finger being tugged at. My wedding ring began to dig into my finger and I moved the ring around so the pain stopped. While I was asleep my wedding ring was taken off my finger. The next day we searched the bedroom from top to bottom but didn't find the ring. We learned later that Moira's father had also had his wedding ring taken in the very same manner. Moira found it outside her front door the day her father died.

May 18th: Before retiring to bed we heard a terrible loud shrill from the flat below our lounge. The lady in question must have been very frightened. We retired to bed and I was awoken by a horrific hand going up my spine. It felt as though it was made of some sort of jelly and I went flying up in the air. It was a horrible, horrible night.

July 9th: Our landlady arrived at the flat. I had telephoned the landlord's secretary to say I wanted to confront her on certain aspects of the paranormal going on in our flat. We did not hold back on asking her if she was aware of the paranormal goings on there. We were shocked to learn that she and the owner of the building were aware of happenings. We gave notice we were quitting the tenancy.

July 14th: I was lifted into the air and moved to the opposite end of the settee. The evening and night became horrendous. The oppressiveness within our flat reached an all time high and Shep became very scared. We stayed in the bedroom until 2am but it got worse. We put on our coats and sat on the local church steps until daylight. When we returned home, the atmosphere was still very bad. We were at the end of our tether.

July 25th: The last pieces of furniture went and Shep and I were alone in the flat. Suddenly I was very aware that all wasn't right. I checked the rooms one last time. I was shocked to discover that the main bedroom had immediately become musty, just as though it hadn't been lived in for about twenty years. As I walked outside with Shep he stopped, looked up at me, and I had this uncanny feeling that like me, it was as though a big weight had been lifted from his mind.

Seven years after leaving the flat, Ed still insists, "Something is radically wrong there. There are ghosts everywhere. It is a deep well of souls. I believe that place is evil. I have no intention of ever going back."

Chapter Twelve

ASSORTMENT OF APPARITIONS

A HEAVY TREAD

The front door opened and closed, footsteps thudded up the stairs. Then came the sounds of cupboards and drawers being opened, slammed shut, and furniture being kicked about. Footsteps in heavy, hobnailed boots stamped around the bedroom for a few minutes before leaving as loudly as they arrived, slamming the front door again.

Vi Perry turned to her daughter, "There, now you've heard it as well. I told you I wasn't imagining things. This house is haunted!"

When Vi moved into Mayfield, a detached Victorian villa in Newport's Fairlee Road, in 1967, she had no idea that she shared her new home with an obstreperous spirit which was heard but never seen. The first time it happened, she thought it was her son, Phil, who had come home for lunch. The next time the ghost made his noisy visit, Vi's daughter heard it all and was as incredulous as her mother.

"It always happened in spring, April or May, and between 11am and noon," said Vi. "My golden retriever who was a very good house dog, heard the ghost. He didn't bark but his hackles went up immediately and he cowered in a corner, looking very frightened, until it had gone. Then he went to the hallway door, sniffing at the air where the ghost had been.

The ghost always followed the same routine - except for the time Vi's sister came to stay. "I don't think he liked her, because he became quite active, making a great deal of noise as though throwing things around and smashing them. Once there was a huge bang and we thought the fridge had exploded, but nothing was ever broken."

It has been a few years since Vi, who is now in her nineties, or her family, have heard the ghost. Whether he has gone for good no-one knows. The house was originally built in 1879 for the Newport station master. It was later bought by the daughter of one of Emma Lady Hamilton's descendants, a certain Miss Douglas-Hamilton, who scandalised polite society and her family, by eloping with her father's coachman. However, the couple never married and did not live happily ever after. Miss Douglas-Hamilton's lover, who took a job on the railway,

A noisy ghost once haunted this house in Fairlee Road, Newport

was killed in a shunting accident, crushed between two wagons. Is it his noisy, restless spirit which was heard at Mayfield - if so, was he in the habit of coming home for lunch between 11am and noon?

PHANTOM FOOTSTEPS

Did building work on a Newport house wake a sleeping ghost? The sound of phantom footsteps often echoed through a house in Clarence Road, once the renovations started. The solid two-storey Victorian terraced house looked ordinary enough from the outside.

Once inside it was a different story, however. But whatever walked was obviously friendly, for the house had a welcoming and quite amiable atmosphere.

Barrie Hamilton of Poleclose Farm, Newport, who bought the house in 1994, first heard those footsteps when he was working alone there one evening. "I was painting in the kitchen when I heard the sound of the front door opening and closing; then footsteps came along the uncarpeted hall towards me, went halfway up the stairs and stopped."

Thinking it was his partner, Sally, arriving, he went into the hall to look for her, but the house was empty.

It was not until both Sally and their builder, Eddie, also experienced those ghostly footfalls when each was alone in the house, that they

Clarence Road at Newport, where ghostly footsteps were heard

realised the place was haunted. Usually the footsteps would occur in the hall and on the landing at about 9pm, although nothing was ever seen.

The house is now occupied by tenants and nothing more has been heard from the ghost. "Perhaps it was the building work which disturbed something in the house. Since the place has been occupied, the footsteps have stopped. All is now quiet there," said Barrie.

GUN HOUSE GHOST

As a girl, Ruth Bennett of Main Road, Arreton, lived in a cottage behind the village pub, the White Lion. Her father was caretaker at nearby St George's Church and it was his responsibility to maintain the churchyard. Next to the church was a dilapidated stone building known locally as the old gun house, where her dad kept his mowers and tools. This has since been renovated as the Arreton Brass Rubbing Centre.

Ruth recalls, "One day when I was eight and my sister was six years old, we were playing among the graves. Through a little window at the rear of the gun house, which was on a level with the churchyard, we could see the figure of a man in there. At first we thought it was a cardboard cut out, as we could only see the back of his head.

"The man was dressed in a long trench coat of dark green, which I later found out was army green. We called out to him but he did not answer or turn around. So we ran round to the front of the gun house where we could see his face.

"It was a pleasant face. He was in his mid-thirties, he wore a flat cap and under his arm he carried a gun. His dark hair was short and he had a moustache. He did not move or even blink, although we were pestering him as children will, asking who he was and what he was doing there.

"Finally we ran to get Dad, but when he came and looked into the gun house he said no-one was there. But the soldier was there because my sister and I could still see him!" (Read more tales of haunted Arreton in Ghosts of the IW Book 4).

The Old Gun House where, two young girls saw the ghost in Army uniform

Chapter Thirteen

DARK SIDE OF THE UNDERCLIFF

THE POP SHOP PHANTOM

A ghost at a 300-year-old cottage at St Lawrence took it rather badly when the owners reluctantly put the place up for sale, doing all it could to persuade the family to stay.

Spring Cottage is a charming old property, which perches just above the road along Undercliff Drive, adjacent to the spring from which it gets its name. At one time the cottage was a 'pop shop' known by local people as 'The Duck', where smuggled wines and brandy could be bought cheaply. This nickname started after a farmer on the Whitwell Road above lost a rare duck from his pond. He first suspected the local fox, but the bedraggled bird emerged days later from the outfall at Spring Cottage, having fallen down the farm well and followed the underground stream to the Undercliff. The duck became something of a local wonder and for many years afterwards people simply called their illicit watering hole 'The Duck'.

When Dinah and Tim Gleed-Owen bought Spring Cottage in 1986, much work was needed to turn the damp and gloomy house into a warm, cosy family home. One bedroom felt particularly sad and

Spring Cottage was once known as 'The Duck'

negative. Dinah, who is especially good at picking up such psychic signals, discovered that an elderly man had died in that room after a long and painful illness. His lonely figure was occasionally glimpsed standing at the window.

Dinah dealt with this by decorating the room in bright primary colours and putting her two young sons in there. The atmosphere changed almost overnight; the spirit was happy to have children in the house and was at peace, she felt.

This state of affairs lasted for almost a decade, during which time Dinah noticed that it became increasingly difficult for her to leave Spring Cottage. Things escalated when the 'For Sale' sign went up. "Every time I tried to go away to the mainland, things would go catastrophically wrong. Fate seemed to conspire to stop me going. People would fall ill, ferries would be cancelled, trains would stop running, cars would break

The 300-year-old Spring Cottage at St Lawrence, pictured in 1994

down, and tickets would disappear. Ever since I have lived here it has been difficult to go away. This seems to be directed particularly at me rather than Tim. It's such an effort to leave that I rarely bother. It is so much easier to stay here. It is clear that the house does not want us to go and is putting obstacles in our way."

The family believed the ghost was somehow responsible, and it was becoming more desperate to keep them there. One of Dinah's sons complained of a dark shape moving about in the bedroom he shared with his brother. The family dogs, dandy dinmonts, which had always been quite happy in the room, took to barking frantically at a wall.

"I know that even when I am by myself here, I am not alone. There is always a presence. I feel someone here. Since we moved in we have become accustomed to small objects, especially jewellery, disappearing, only to turn up weeks, months or even years later. Floorboards upstairs creak with the tread of invisible feet, but it is not at all frightening. This is a happy house, a busy house, filled with children and people and I believe that our unseen presence enjoys having us here," said Dinah. "It is quite a compliment that it doesn't want us to leave."

But the house was eventually sold and the family moved to Yorkshire. Retired schoolteacher and former Island councillor, Robin Ford, who bought Spring Cottage in 1996 hasn't been troubled by the supernatural since. "The place creaks a bit at night, what old house doesn't? Ghosts? I don't believe in them," he smiled.

SPIRITS AT THE OLD INN

The St Lawrence Inn, which perches at the side of the Ventnor Undercliff, has a long history as a staging post and coaching inn for weary travellers. At one time it was used as the public bar to the Carfax Hotel tap next door, and was split into four tiny bar rooms. Built on several levels, there was stabling beneath the main inn and later, part of the building was used as the village fire station. There were double doors fronting the road and the floor was reinforced to support the weight of the little fire engine.

With its long and chequered history, it is hardly surprising that several licensees and their families have, in recent years, had some strange experiences there. One of the most dramatic of these was witnessed by Andrew Lloyd when his parents, June and Alan, owned the pub. Now manager of the Island branch of a finance company, Andrew still remembers quite vividly the night he awoke to see a man's figure emerge from the floor and rise through the room, disappearing by way of the ceiling.

"I was sleeping in one of the attic rooms at the time. Something woke me and I became aware that I was not alone. I could see a man's figure rising from the floor. It went on up and up to the ceiling then disappeared. I could see it was a man with a bearded face who was slightly transparent. Middle-aged with dark hair, he had a big smile on

The St Lawrence Inn pictured in 1994

his face. But, he only had half a body; I could not see any legs at all. His figure ended at the waist. I kept my eyes fixed on him as he rose up through the room. This took perhaps half a minute before he vanished into the roof," said Andrew.

This was not his only supernatural experience at the old inn. His mother, June, recalled that when the family moved there in the mid-1980s, Andrew stayed in a flat under the oldest part of the building. But he soon complained he was being woken at 3am by the sound of footsteps running around overhead in the children's room - although the place was locked and empty.

A snooker table in that room, which June described as 'a great heavy thing' would be moved in the night, only a matter of inches, but always enough to need pushing back into place. "That room was never really warm," said June. "Even with a roaring fire going in there it was cold. Often when I was locking up I could feel an icy wall there."

Perhaps the ghostly figure, which glides down the passageway into that room, has something to do with that unnatural chill. When June saw it one night, all she could make out was a pale blue shape, obviously female, moving slowly into the children's room. There it vanished, much to the consternation of the pub dogs.

Soon after they moved into the inn, June's former husband found a blocked-up window inside an old cupboard in one of the back bedrooms. The frame was visible and the window itself had been boarded in with wood. "He came for the crowbar to unblock it as he was curious to see what was behind. A few minutes later he was back, his face ashen. The cupboard was empty. That window frame had vanished! He wouldn't go into that room for months after that," said June.

Gill Pepperell, who ran the St Lawrence Inn with her family a few years earlier, often sensed a presence in the kitchens and the bathroom.

The Inn at St Lawrence re-opened at Easter 2000 after being extensively renovated

"I would feel that there was someone behind me or brushing past me, but when I turned to look, nothing was there. My children hated their attic bedrooms and insisted on sleeping together in the same room. They were always making excuses to stay at friends' houses, or at the family's other home in the village. They had no regrets when we left the inn," said Gill.

One of the pub ghosts was reputed to be the spirit of a former landlady and Gill's mother was able to describe her clearly after a brief encounter in the bar one morning. While polishing the counter before opening, she saw an elderly lady standing at the far end of the room. Gill's mother called out, "Sorry, we're not open yet, dear."

The lady wore a high-necked blouse with a brooch at the throat, an old-fashioned long skirt and her white hair was scraped back into a bun. She looked so very pale that Gill's mother went after her thinking she must be ill, but the old lady completely disappeared. When Gill described what had happened to some of the regulars, they told her it was the ghost of a former landlady keeping an eye on the place.

A pub spirit was no novelty for landlord Craige Turland, who took on the St Lawrence Inn with partner Kay Verden in 1994 - for he once ran what was reputed to be the most haunted pub in Northants. He never met the old landlady's ghost, although customers told him she was still around. And most mornings when he went into the children's room, his first job would be to move that snooker table a few inches - back into its proper place. When the St Lawrence Inn closed in 1995, villagers feared they had lost their local for good. However, at Easter 2000, it re-opened as The Inn at St Lawrence, a free house run as a family concern, with

James Collins as licensee. Soon after they moved there in 1997, the family quickly became aware of both ghosts. Fortunately, James's aunt, Sue Robertson, is psychic and has been able to communicate with their restless spirits. That of the former landlady, she and fellow psychic Margo Williams have succeeded in moving on 'towards the light'; the other, a stablehand named Jeremiah Smith has not yet found peace, remaining earthbound at the inn.

Ghost with a roving eye

"The ghostly old lady was not a nice spirit. Very authoritarian and strict, she did not like people and was particularly annoyed when children or animals came to 'her' inn. She had a very strong presence and still regarded the whole place as hers. She was determined to stay and keep control, so it was not easy to persuade her to move on. She had to learn to like people before she could do so," said Sue.

The ghostly Jeremiah, who was raised as an Irish Catholic, has proved to be more of a challenge. Something of a ladies' man, Jeremiah worked as stable hand at the inn during Victorian times and was also in charge of the village fire engine. His roving eye was his downfall and after an unhappy affair with a local woman, he apparently threw himself down the well. Suicide was, for him, a mortal sin; Jeremiah's unhappy soul is still in self-imposed purgatory, despite Sue's best efforts.

This impudent spirit is still fond of the ladies and sometimes makes his presence known by fondling them or pinching bottoms. At one dinner party a guest was pushed face-first into her food, while Jeremiah stroked another female guest on the leg. "He's a bit of a dirty old man really, but he is learning to behave himself better now. He has kept an eye on all the building work and often followed James around, moving tools, stacking and tidying them away when James was trying to use them," said Sue. "I think Jeremiah approves of what has been done to the inn - he's often around, but he keeps his hands to himself now!"

MORE TALES FROM THE HAUNTED HOSPITAL

It has been more than 30 years since the old Royal National Hospital at Ventnor was demolished and Ventnor Botanic Gardens rose, phoenix-like, from the rubble. But the hospital, where more than 100,000 patients were treated for consumption, did not give in gracefully. Its death throes brought ghost hunters and psychic investigators from all over the world.

Psychic activity was centred very strongly around the old operating theatre which was virtually the last part of the building to be torn down. Long after the rest of the hospital was reduced to rubble, that operating theatre held out, defying attempts to knock it down by mechanical means. Four tractors, excavators and a ball and crane were wrecked in the attempt.

Finally, the job was given to two workmen with sledgehammers. They however, complained of a young, ghostly girl who would stand staring at them as they worked. Nearby residents complained constantly. Not about the dust and noise from the demolition work, but about the moaning, weeping and groaning, coming from the empty building at night. Grey misty shapes were seen flitting about the ruins, and the workmen complained of feeling icy cold there, even as they wielded sledgehammers. (Read their stories in More Ghosts of the IW, and of the haunted hospital's reappearance in Book 4)

At last the site was levelled and a car park built on top. But strange things continued to happen. Despite a service of exorcism by local clergy, ghosts continued to make their presence felt. A four-inch thick, armour-plated power cable buried in a trench running across the operating theatre site suddenly stopped functioning, cutting off power to the Garden Tavern. When the trench was opened up, electricity board workers found the thick cable had been neatly chopped into 2ft 6in lengths. How it was done and by whom was never discovered.

With the car park surfaced over, few visitors now realise there was ever a hospital on the site. But the operating theatre still exerts a malign and disturbing influence. Some dogs grow agitated, refusing to walk across that area of the car park. Staff have noticed there are an unusually high number of accidents there - if a child falls and cuts a knee, or someone trips and sprains an ankle, it will be in that area.

A warm August night

Cars, too, are affected, breaking down or refusing to start there with surprising regularity.

It was a warm August night in 1990 when Tony Ewington and his family stopped off at Ventnor Botanic Gardens for a drink at the Garden Tavern. After an agreeable evening, they returned to the car which had been parked near the top of the path, but it refused to start. Everything was dead. There were no lights; the electrical system was lifeless. Nothing would work.

Psychic activity continues long after the Royal National Hospital was demolished

At a loss and wondering what to do next, Tony lifted the bonnet and fiddled with the wiring in the vain hope that it would somehow make things better. It didn't. He finally got back into the car to consult with the others, but as he did so, Tony noticed smoke filling the passenger compartment. He shouted at everyone to get out immediately and run from the car, fearing it was about to burst into flames.

When he looked back from a safe distance however, there was no sign of smoke. His puzzled family asked what the matter was, for they had not seen or smelled anything. Finally, they pushed the car across the car park to where there was some illumination to have a better look at the problem. As Tony opened the door, the interior light came on and when he tried the ignition, the car started immediately. It was not until he was driving home that Tony realised the vehicle had been parked on the site of that old operating theatre...

Power Plants and Bulbs

May 2000 saw the opening of a £1.5 million Millennium visitor centre at the Botanic Gardens. This splendid new building leads from the car park (close to the site of the old operating theatre) to the Garden Tavern. It replaces a sloping path which was known by patients - and not with affection - as "Haemorrhage Hill". If you could walk up this without

The hospital, which closed in the 1960's, is now the site of Ventnor Botanic Gardens

relapsing, you were well on the way to being cured, it was said.

However, since the new centre's official opening by botanist Dr David Bellamy, problems with the electrical systems there have not gone unnoticed by curator, Simon Goodenough. As well as power failures and a number of visits by the fire brigade to release people trapped in the centre's new lift system, Simon is astounded at the number of light bulbs which fail there. "It's not just the odd bulb we have to replace, it can be 40 or 50 at a time. The contractors however, can find no logical reason for this!"

For decades there has been an extraordinary level of supernatural activity surrounding the old hospital itself and latterly its site. Demolition of the building has not diminished the number or frequency of ghostly manifestations there, for the very place has a curious energy of its own.

On a warm sunny day among the exotic shrubs and trees - with other visitors never far away - talk of ghosts or hauntings is easily dismissed as the product of an over-active imagination. But as dusk approaches, the last visitors leave and birds fall silent. There is something disquieting about the very stillness. As shadows lengthen, then melt into darkness, the gardens belong to the ghosts once more.

Towngate Bridge, at the foot of Hunnyhill, was formerly a main road into Newport

Chapter Fourteen

HAUNTED HUNNYHILL

The name Hunny Hill which dates back to the thirteenth century, comes from the Old English hunig hyll, meaning 'the hill where wild honey could be gathered'

THE NEWSAGENT GHOST

For many years it has been a newsagent's shop, and formerly a haberdashery and fruit shop. C&C News is certainly a long-established part of the community at Newport's Towngate Bridge at the foot of Hunnyhill. Now run by Cliff and Cheryl Carter, it is a busy shop with many regular customers and the family live above the premises in a three-storey building, which dates back more than 150 years.

Since moving there in 1980, they have made considerable alterations to the living accommodation, but have not been able to do anything about a mischievous, light-fingered presence which cannot resist small objects left around the shop. Keys are a favourite target and on one memorable occasion the sole shop key went missing, only to turn up later inside a teacup on the kitchen table. Rings and other small pieces of Cheryl's jewellery disappear for days or weeks, reappearing in strange places; one watch even turned up in the bottom of her wardrobe.

"I get a sense of something around me and I feel it is a child," said Cheryl. "Staff are always complaining of things being moved in the shop, while upstairs in a passageway at the top of the staircase, there is sometimes a feeling of coldness and of a presence there. It certainly doesn't bother us though."

Less pleasant memories

Jo Mayes, who lived over the shop with her parents and sister for almost ten years, has less pleasant memories of her time there. Jo, who now resides with her husband and children in New Street, Newport, recalls, "Mum and Dad bought the business in 1963 and Mum ran it as Brady's Newsagents. I remember there was a particular place on the first floor, a corridor where odd things happened. It was always cold there, you could never get warm and the hairs on the back of your neck would rise as you walked along there. We would hear odd noises, knocking and banging. Whenever something bad was about to happen these sounds would increase in frequency and the knocks would grow louder and louder.

"Before we moved to the Island, Dad had a cancer operation in London. Sadly when the cancer returned, that knocking and hammering began in earnest. It seemed to be coming from the air around us, we could never discover where; the noise just got worse and worse. Dad was at home until the week before he died and by this time those awful sounds were incredibly loud. When he died, they stopped instantly.

"My grandmother lived with us at this time and her bedroom was on the first floor, by that corridor. She often

The haunted newsagent's shop

said she could hear people moving about in the corridor and the sounds of long, old-fashioned skirts rustling against the walls outside her room. Those knocks started again when my grandmother fell and broke her hip. She was really frightened and told my mother, 'They've come for me this time.'

"Mother had had enough and put the place up for sale. I think it really scared her. My grandmother refused to stay there and insisted on going into a nursing home instead. She never returned to the shop and died in 1971.

"My sister and I slept in the attic bedrooms on the top floor and hardly heard the knocking sounds, but both my parents and my grandmother certainly did. As they grew in intensity, the banging, thudding noises seemed to surround them, reverberating about the walls."

As a child of six or seven, Jo recalls catching fleeting glimpses of a woman dressed in old-fashioned, long dresses, moving about the place. "I heard the rustling noises too, and we would often lose small trinkets, jewellery and keys, especially keys."

PHANTOM IN A LEATHER APRON

Fortunately Cheryl and Cliff have never had occasion to hear that awful knocking in the dead of night, but Cheryl had another haunting experience just a few doors away at Number 1, Lower St James' Street, Newport. It happened when she and Cliff were living above the old-established butcher's shop of E. E. Downer for several years in the early 1980s while renovating the accommodation above their own shop.

"I was on the landing when I looked down to see a young baby toddling unsteadily along. It was a very blonde, fair-skinned child in an old-fashioned terry nappy and it was trailing something behind it, a blanket, or shawl perhaps, I couldn't really tell. The ghost-child stayed there for a few brief moments before vanishing in front of me," recalled Cheryl. "I never saw him again, but he was a rather beautiful baby."

E. E. Downer is one of the last remaining independent butchers in the town and Greg Downer, who has run the family business for years, is well aware that his shop is haunted - but he has never seen that ethereal spirit-child.

He and fellow butcher Dave Lockyer have heard the unmistakable noise of footsteps in a passageway at the back of the shop, as well as what sounds like a heavy, long leather apron - the sort an old-fashioned slaughterman would have worn - slapping against those stout work boots.

Both men are also rather embarrassed to have been interrupted while in the WC by a ghostly hand rattling the door. "Something definitely walks along the passageway with very heavy footsteps and tries the door. You can see the handle turn and the door moves, although it is latched," said Dave. "The first time it happened in the summer of 1999 I thought it must be the boss, but he was in the shop with a customer. Then on another occasion the very same thing happened to him!

A slaughterman's ghost still walks here in Newport

"This has been a butcher's shop for well over a century - since about the 1870s, and I think in those days there was a slaughterhouse on the premises in what is now our fridge room at the back," said Greg.

Meanwhile, in the shop itself, fine old Victorian ceramic tiles adorn the walls while the original rows of chrome hooks for hanging meat remain. And at night, when the shop is closed and empty, the distinctive sound of these hooks moving on their rails can sometimes still be heard, as they are pushed by an unseen hand.

LITTLE SHOP OF SPIRITS

The following story concerns a property in Newport, which was for many years one of the showrooms for Frank Cheverton's motor dealership. In the 1970s the business moved to premises at Riverway and the building was sold. Fearful perhaps that mention of stray spirits there may frighten nervous customers, the mainland-based owners who are part of a national chain, unfortunately do not want their shop identified. Therefore, names have been changed ... to protect the ghosts!

In the year 1852 cabinet maker, William Cheverton, started in business as a coach builder and repairer at Broadlands, Newport. Chevertons were soon well-known for their carriages and once Royal patronage from Queen Victoria's household at Osborne was secured, orders came pouring in for other special vehicles, including bathing carriages, snow sleighs and barouches. And as the new century dawned, the family woke to the potential of horseless carriages - although when young Frank A. Cheverton opened a Motor Department in 1904 - there were just 17 motor cars on the Isle of Wight!

Ultimately, Chevertons grew to encompass nearly an acre of central Newport between Lugley Street and Crocker Street, while the firm employed more than 100 people. For more than half a century, gleaming new models graced that showroom, but it finally closed in the 1970s when new owners, Premier Ford, moved the business to larger premises.

Whatever haunts that former car showroom has done so for some time. Tom Skeats of Carisbrooke worked for many years in the parts department which was situated in an upstairs storeroom. He recalls, "It was quite a creepy place, especially at night. For a time I lived next door and if we were busy I would sometimes go back and work there alone of an evening. I never actually saw anything, but upstairs things would

The spare parts stores where ghostly activity was seen at night

fall about for no reason. Tools and motor parts would jump up out of their trays then fall to the floor making quite a racket.

After Chevertons had moved, a mainland chain took over the building. One manager who was there for six years admits that the Newport shop was the strangest place he has ever worked in. It started with shadows and noises in the empty storeroom above the shop. Heavy trolleys would move across the room by themselves. Shelving would fall to pieces suddenly. A heap of staff forms left on a desk one night were sorted through by unseen hands and left in a neat pile, in date order.

"The premises had excellent security, but sometimes, for no reason, the alarm wouldn't set properly or would go off in that upstairs room. One night, when I was there on my own, the noises upstairs became so bad that I thought we had an intruder and called the police.

"The noises were still going on when they arrived, but although officers searched everywhere they couldn't find out where the sounds were coming from. They joked that we must have a ghost!" he said.

Freeze-frame ghost

"One night our video security system stopped on freeze-frame showing the figure of a woman. The video had been recording, but there was nothing else on the tape. The screen just froze on this dark image.

"Although the noises were loudest upstairs, the weirdest feelings were in the kitchen and office downstairs, where you would feel the sensation of an unseen presence with you."

However, when the manager left for the mainland in November 1997, he thought it best not to mention to new manager, Annie, that the premises were haunted. Annie, who plays for the Island's women's rugby team, is not easily scared, so when staff told her there was a

The interior of the Ford showrooms in 1952

ghost in the building, she thought they were having a laugh. "But on 14 February 1998, I was in the upstairs toilet at 11am when I heard two loud bangs coming from the front of the shop. I ran down but could find nothing wrong. At 3pm the shop was empty so I went into the office. Sitting at the desk, I heard someone in the shop open and slam the front door. I checked the security camera but there was no one there. After that, whatever was there became very active," said Annie.

One night she was called out at 2am because the intruder alarm had gone off. "The sensor that triggered the alarm was at the front of the building in the upstairs store room above the shop, in the area where the noises were coming from. It was in this area that a white, misty shape was seen by a member of staff." After this, Annie started to keep a diary of odd events at the shop.

Diary of a Haunting

21 February: Constant feelings of being watched. Atmosphere building up, it seems charged with energy.

1 March: Noises of cups being moved in the kitchen sink. Staff reluctant to work on their own now.

9 March: Tony heard a dull thud from upstairs and felt cold spots in the office. After hearing a very loud bang overhead he rang to ask me to come in, as he was too afraid to stay on his own. He was standing ashen-faced by the door when I arrived.

12 March: David who was working the stockroom heard a bang and thumping, stamping sounds going up and down the stairs. The office

The former Ford showrooms where ghosts still walk

felt very cold and he heard a loud bang above the office.

18 March: The sound of heavy footsteps heard moving about overhead, directly above the tills between 6.30pm and 10.30pm.

19 March: Strong smell of oranges in the shop near the tills. At 9.30pm the chill cabinet door opened and shut. Banging noises from upstairs.

20 March: Loud bangs from upstairs above tills.

22 March: Rustling sounds and tuneless whistling coming from kitchen at 9pm.

23 March: Foul smell (like sewage) near chill cabinet. Heavy stomping sounds upstairs. Lights flickering.

25 March: Felt strong wave of emotion and burst into tears for no reason. Sitting at the desk in the office, without warning an intense sense of sadness swept through me. I felt someone was in there with me. I left quickly. At 6pm Tony smelled oranges at the back of the shop near the till.

1 April: Ivy, a local psychic and medium, arrived to try to find out what was haunting the building. She sensed the presence of a man who didn't like women, but was unable to move him on. He was too strong for her.

25 April: Wooden door to upstairs toilet is locked from the inside. Unable to get it open. David said he heard moaning sounds there.

26 April: Door is still locked. Sounds of shuffling and scraping noises. David and John heard noises again. Think an animal must be trapped in there.

28 April: Toilet door is unlocked! Opens freely. No key there. Only a latch on the inside.

29 April: Toilet door locked again. Weird noise like a baby or very young child whimpering and what I can only describe as the sound of a single, old-fashioned windscreen wiper squeaking or scraping on a dry, but greasy windscreen. Both noises heard by other staff too. I rang the police immediately. Police officer arrived and we locked the shop. He stomped upstairs in his heavy boots. The noises from the toilet stopped. He put his head towards the door then both noises started again.

He said, "Police. Open the Door". The noises continued. He said, "It's the Police. Open the door or I will have to break it open." The noises carried on.

He kicked the door. It opened. We all expected to see something but the room was empty. Nothing to see. The window was still locked. Nothing. I was disappointed. The policeman was surprised. He said it must have been wind making the noises. But it wasn't windy. He checked the rest of the building. Then he said, "This is one for the X Files, I reckon."

One for the X-Files....

Annie rang Wilma, another psychic, from Bembridge. "As I spoke to her on the 'phone, the temperature in the office dropped sharply and I could feel something in there with me," said Annie.

Wilma sensed that the old building was haunted by the spirit of a man who remained earthbound because he was still attached to money in the building. "He despises women and treated them badly when he was alive," she added.

"Wilma attempted to move him on and when she had finished, that upstairs room felt fine; full of positive energy. Between May and October we hardly had any problems, apart from smells of old-fashioned tobacco or cigar smoke which wafted around the shop sometimes, while the lights flickered on and off."

By October however, activity was beginning again. The vacuum cleaner suddenly started up, although it was switched off at the wall; bottles were found smashed in a locked room and the feeling of being watched was intensifying. On Friday 30 October, Annie was cashing up when the lights suddenly went out. "I had to go back into the office for my wallet, but as I reached for it, something told me to leave immediately. 'This is my time. Get out of my space' it seemed to be saying. It was very unpleasant. I rang Wilma, and she told me that other spirits were passing through the building."

Although the presence in the shop has often been heard, rarely is anything seen. David once saw the outline of an old lady in Victorian costume standing downstairs, just above floor level, near the staircase. While Annie once encountered a presence which was standing barring the door to the office. "I walked through him to get in. The air felt cold and heavy, as if the air pressure was charged. He was a large man, for my head went through his chest and shoulders," she shuddered.

The haunting continued sporadically, with footsteps, noises, smells and staff reporting the sensation of an unseen presence. When Annie left in December 1999 to manage a store in Ryde, it was with a great feeling of relief. "I felt as though a cloud had lifted," she confessed.

Author's note: While researching this haunting at the request of the Society for Psychical Research, I discovered that the premises were once two separate shops which were knocked into one and extensively altered in the 1950s. One of these was owned by Chevertons; for almost a century the other belonged to the Wapshott family who ran a greengrocer's shop there. Could this account for the strong smell of oranges which staff noticed at the rear of this side of the shop?

A MONK IN PRAYER

The services of two Newport priests were needed to help deal with a ghostly monk haunting a brand new house, one of a terrace of three, in Vicarage Walk, just off Hunnyhill.

The year was 1972 and Maureen Collins had just given birth to baby Steven at nearby St Mary's Hospital. She explained, "When I returned home with Steven I was aware that the atmosphere in the house changed. It would suddenly become very cold and I had the feeling that there was 'something' in the room with me. Initially I put it down to the strangeness of having a new baby, even wondering if it was the start of post-natal depression or the baby blues. My husband was at work all day and I was on my own with the baby most of the time."

However Maureen, who now lives with husband, Bill, at Coombe Park, Wroxall, realised her intuition had been correct when she saw the tall figure of a monk wearing a black habit. He was standing in the front room, leaning over the baby's cot. "He turned to look at me, although I could not see his face because it was hidden by his cowl. In his hands was an open prayer book. As I stepped forward he drifted through the bedroom wall into the next door house.

"After that I saw him at least a couple of times a week. He would appear, then lean over Steven and me. In a curious way I found it rather

Old Towngate Mill at the foot of Hunnyhill

comforting. Steven was not well at the time as there was problem with his feeding. I believe that the monk's spirit was praying for him and had come to help protect him," said Maureen.

The ghost would usually appear in her front room at 10am, heralding his arrival with a feeling of intense cold. He always carried that prayer book with him; sometimes open, sometimes clasped shut. Occasionally he would open it while looking at Maureen and the baby.

"I hesitated to say anything to anybody about this because I thought I was going quite mad," said Maureen. Then hairdresser, Maz Powder, who lived next door, came round one day to do her hair. Suddenly Maz burst into floods of tears. "When I asked what the matter was, Maz said that her husband, Ray, was refusing to stay in the house because a ghost in the bedroom had tried to suffocate him! The atmosphere in that room had grown so oppressive that Ray had been unable to breathe."

I couldn't open my eyes

Maz and Ray, who now live in Melville Gardens, Sandown, recall that incident all too clearly. "I woke up suddenly in the night. There was a threatening presence in the room. I could hardly breathe; the air felt thick and cloying," shuddered Ray. "I couldn't open my eyes no matter how much I struggled, they were sealed shut. It was terrifying."

Beside him, Maz, too, woke in a cold sweat, unable to move. "I was aware of a presence in the room with us but I could see nothing. I always wore a crucifix and tried to put my hand to my neck to touch it. But my hand wouldn't move; it felt like I was paralysed. The house was new when we moved in, so we were more than a little surprised to discover it was haunted. I was aware of a presence on a number of occasions, although I never saw anything. However, it was not until I talked to Maureen that I discovered her house was haunted too."

Bless this house

Maureen continued, "In a way, I was pleased that I was not alone in seeing the ghost. It had never harmed me or Steven, but if it was frightening people, I knew something had to be done." Maureen, who was raised as Roman Catholic, contacted both her local priest, Father Quinn, and Vicar of Newport, the Reverend James Buckett.

"Reverend Buckett visited first, blessing the houses from outside. Although the monk's appearances grew fewer, he was still there, so Father Quinn came round to move the ghost on and cleanse the houses.

"Whatever he did, it worked, for I never saw the monk again, although I sometimes sensed his presence, especially if Steven was unwell. And Steven would sometimes tell me had been talking to 'the man with white hair'."

Although those houses at Vicarage Walk were new, the land they occupied once belonged to one of Newport's ancient religious houses, the twelfth century Priory of St Cross. The Priory, which pre-dates the town had its own water mill, was used as a hospital and had a licence for burying its own dead.

This facility was needed when, according to legend, two of the monks had a fierce quarrel and one of the men cut the throat of the other with a pair of scissors. The murderer dropped the weapon onto a flagstone, which was stained with the victim's lifeblood. Though the guilty monk, whose hair apparently turned white overnight, had to try every day to obliterate the stains as a penance, they could never be removed....

Was the figure, seen by Maureen and baby Steven, the earthbound shade of that unhappy monk? If so, he may now have found peace, thanks to the efforts and prayers of two twentieth century priests.

Vicarage Walk is directly opposite Brook View Cottage at the bottom of Hunnyhill, where the ghost of a grey-haired old lady was regularly seen. Ivy Early moved to the cottage upon her marriage, living there for more than 50 years until her death in 1972. She was housebound with arthritis when she died there in her eighties. But for years afterwards, Ivy Early's shade would appear at the window, gazing wistfully out at her back garden.

THE VICTORIAN RAILWAYMAN'S SPECTRE

Late at night when the town is still and silent, a long-dead railwayman lights his lamp and sets out to check that the sidings at Newport Station are secure. His phantom figure is seen and heard as he makes his rounds, lantern swinging at his side.

The old station, which stood at the northern end of Holyrood Street, has long since been swept away to be replaced by a series of road junctions, an electrical superstore, and car dealerships.

Although no trains have run there since the 1960s, a ghostly steam locomotive pulling three spectral carriages once materialised briefly - in broad daylight - to Kay Liggens of Freshwater, who glimpsed it crossing an old bridge at the bottom of Holyrood Street.

The phantom railwayman's figure has been seen by a number of staff at Premier Motors on Riverway Industrial Estate, while others have heard him rattling doors as if making sure they are secure. Service manager, Robert LeBrecht, was working late one night when he encountered the ghost in what he has always sensed to be "a dark and nasty part of the building".

"I heard the door rattling and looked up. I thought at first that we had an intruder, for there in the corner was a man wearing a Victorian-style railwayman's flat cap and overalls. He swung a lantern at his side as he moved. I realised he was a ghost when I saw him walk through the door without opening it!"

"Over the years he has been seen about the place by quite a number of staff and has given a few of them quite a fright. We were curious to know what he was doing here and when we did some research, we discovered that Premier Motors was built on the site of the former sidings of the Newport, Yarmouth and Freshwater Railway."

This delightful, scenic line opened in 1888, closing in 1953. Relations with the IW Central Railway were often acrimonious, and when Central closed Newport station to Freshwater trains in 1913, the smaller company immediately built its own ramshackle station a few yards down the line!

A Victorian railwayman's ghost is still seen at the former sidings of the Newport, Yarmouth and Freshwater Railway, although the site is now Premier Motors

In 1923 the companies were absorbed by the Southern Railway, which later became British Railways. Sadly, the last traces of the little Newport, Yarmouth and Freshwater branch line have now vanished. In 1998, the old brick viaduct arches near St Cross Mill and the ramshackle shed which served as the ticket office, were swept away in the name of progress, to be replaced by a road servicing a supermarket and petrol station.

But that ghostly railwayman hasn't noticed, for he exists in a dark dimension of his own, where steam trains still run...

THE END

BIBLIOGRAPHY

AND FURTHER READING

Kokeritz, Helge - The Place-names of the Isle of Wight.

Eldridge, R.J. - Newport in Bygone Days.

Shepard, Bill - Newport Remembered.

Hassell - Tour of the Isle of Wight.

Bullar, John - Guide to the Isle of Wight, 1821.

Cooke's Isle of Wight, 1813.

Winter, C.W.R. - This Enchanted Isle.

Cox, J.Charles - Country Churches of the Isle of Wight.

Albin - Companian or Vectiana, 1806.

Mitchell, Kevin - Newport Pubs.

Searle, Adrian - Isle of Wight Folklore.

Searle, Adrian - Isle of Wight at War.

Mudie's Hampshire.

Brading, Rosetta - West Cowes and Northwood.

Jones, Jack and Johanna - The Isle of Wight, An Illustrated History.

Garle, Hubert - A Driving Tour of the Isle of Wight.

Tatem and Opie - A Dictionary of Superstitions.

Underwood, Peter - Ghosts and How to See Them.

Worsley, Richard - A History of the Isle of Wight, 1781.

J.W. Hill and Co, IW Directory, 1871.

L.B. Taylor - The Ghosts of Virginia.

Nancy Roberts - South Carolina Ghosts.

THE AUTHOR

Gay Baldwin began researching and recording ghost stories in 1977, when the first book, *Ghosts of the Isle of Wight*, written with Ray Anker was published. There is certainly no shortage of hauntings on the Island, and *More Ghosts of the Isle of Wight, Ghosts of the Isle of Wight III* and *Isle of Wight Ghosts Book 4*, have also been local best sellers.

She devised the popular Island Ghost Walks, a series of historical walks with a supernatural slant, which have introduced thousands of Islanders and visitors to the darker side of towns such as Newport and Cowes.

Although not psychic herself, as a journalist who is also a member of the Ghost Club Society, Gay has interviewed many hundreds of people who have incredible and inexplicable experiences of hauntings. Armed with the facts she then researches the history of the sites or houses involved, looking for reasons for the ghostly happenings.

Some accounts defy rational explanation and this fifth book of Isle of Wight ghost stories will give even the most confirmed sceptic pause for thought.

Some of the things that go bump in the night are easily explained away. An over-active imagination can conjure up all sorts of "ghostly" sounds, smells and apparitions. Creaking timbers, skeletal branches tap tapping on window panes, owls or bats in flight after dark; mice or rats scurrying through attics or behind walls, can be the innocent origin of many a ghost story. Not in every case however....

After more than twenty years of writing about ghosts, Gay firmly believes in the supernatural. Too many people, reasonable, rational, sensible people, have had experiences and encounters which cannot be explained away by anything other than supernatural means.

Gay would like to hear any strange tales of ghosts or hauntings that you might have. She can be contacted by phone on: (01983) 294651, or by e-mail on gb@hauntediw.demon.co.uk

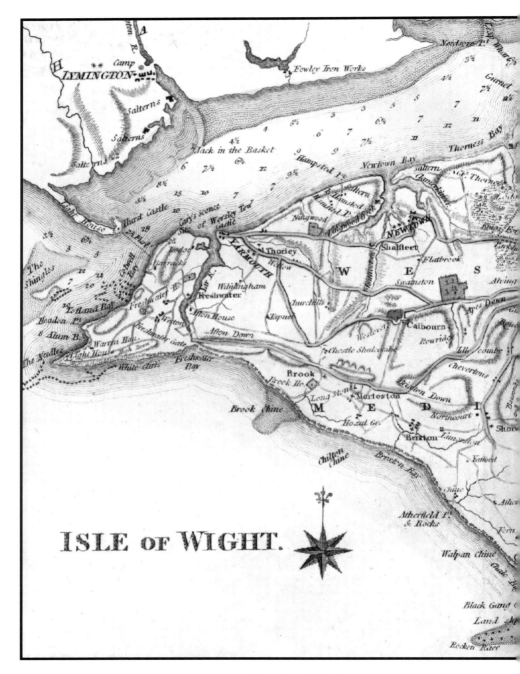

A map of the Isle of Wight

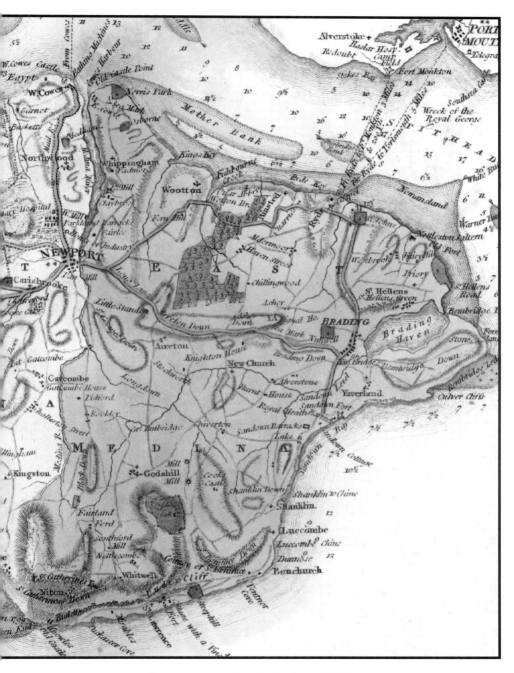

From an engraving by Cooke in 1808

This short check-list for ghost-hunters is based on a Society for Psychical Research guide to investigating hauntings.
If you want to go ghost-hunting, don't trespass on private property, take a friend, a camera, go with an open mind, and remember:
There's nothing quite so funny as the idea of a ghost...until you happen to meet one!

Name: .... Current age: .... Occupation: ....

Address: ....

Location of encounter: ....

Time and date(s) of encounter: ....

Weather conditions: .... Lighting conditions: ....

Distance from apparition: .... Witnesses present: ....

Was the ghost fully or partially visible? If so describe its:

shape, size, colour and appearance: ....

Was it opaque: .... shadowy: .... solid: ....

Was it male: .... female: .... child: .... animal: ....

What was the ghost wearing? ....

How long did the phenomenon last? ....

Was the ghost in motion: .... If so, how did it move: ....

Did it pass through any solid object including walls, doors or people? ....

Did it make any noise (i.e. bangings, footsteps, sobbing)? ....

Did the ghost speak: .... What was said: ....

Was the ghost aware of your presence? ....

Did you notice a rise or fall in temperature: ....

Did you recognise the ghost as a deceased person? ....

Did the ghost frighten you? ....

Were any animals present: .... How did they react: ....

Does the ghost appear regularly? ....

Is there any pattern to the appearances? ....

Are objects moved: .... Do objects disappear/appear: ....

Does the ghost affect electrical equipment or machinery? ....

Do you notice any smell: .... What is it: ....

Does the site have a history of hauntings? ....

NOT SPOOKED YET ?

WHY NOT ORDER YOUR PERSONAL, AUTOGRAPHED COPIES OF THE OTHER BOOKS IN THIS SERIES. THEY ALSO MAKE THOUGHTFUL GIFTS FOR NERVOUS FRIENDS !!

Photocopy or send this order form to :
Gay Baldwin
9 Pine Tree Close
Cowes, Isle of Wight
PO31 8DX
Telephone : (01983) 294651 : e-mail gb@hauntediw.demon.co.uk

....	copies of **Ghosts of the IW**	@ **£4.95 each**	£..............
....	copies of **More Ghosts of the IW**	@ **£4.95 each**	£..............
....	copies of **Ghosts of the IW book III**	@ **£6.95 each**	£..............
....	copies of **IW Ghosts, book four**	@ **£6.95 each**	£..............
....	copies of **Ghost Island, book five**	@ **£7.95 each**	£..............

Add £1.00 postage and packing for the first book and 75p for each additional book.

	Postage	£..............
	TOTAL	£..............

Please make cheque/postal order payable to : Gay Baldwin.

NOTE: I usually dispatch orders the same or next day. Please allow 28 days before you panic. If a book _has_ to be somewhere by a certain date, let me know so I can try to get it there on time.

You can also buy on line at www.ghost-island.com

Now also available - the Isle of Wight Ghost Hunter's map at £1.00 each with postage 20p.

Name   ....

Address   ....

....Post Code ....

Telephone ....e-mail ....

Check out new stories on www.ghost-island.com